60 Cajun and Creole Recipes for Home

By: Kelly Johnson

Table of Contents

Appetizers:

- Cajun Shrimp and Grits
- Crab-Stuffed Mushrooms
- Creole Deviled Eggs
- Crawfish Étouffée Stuffed Jalapeños
- Boudin Balls with Remoulade Sauce
- Andouille Sausage Sliders with Creole Mustard

Soups and Gumbos:

- Chicken and Sausage Gumbo
- Seafood Okra Gumbo
- Shrimp and Corn Bisque
- Creole Chicken and Sausage Soup
- Red Beans and Rice Soup
- Oyster and Artichoke Soup

Main Dishes - Seafood:

- Blackened Catfish
- Jambalaya with Shrimp, Chicken, and Andouille Sausage
- Shrimp Creole
- Crawfish Pie
- Cajun Grilled Lobster Tails
- Creole Crab Cakes

Main Dishes - Poultry:

- Chicken and Andouille Sausage Étouffée
- Bourbon Street Chicken
- Creole Roast Chicken
- Smothered Turkey Wings
- Cajun Stuffed Chicken Breast
- Turkey and Sausage Gumbo

Main Dishes - Meat:

- Cajun Boudin Sausage
- Pork Grillades and Grits
- Cajun Meat Pies
- Creole Beef Daube
- Andouille and Chicken Jambalaya
- Dirty Rice with Ground Beef and Pork

Side Dishes:

- Cajun Corn Maque Choux
- Creole Mustard Potato Salad
- Red Beans and Rice
- Collard Greens with Andouille
- Cajun Dirty Rice
- Baked Macaroni and Cheese

Vegetarian/Vegan:

- Vegan Gumbo
- Cajun-Style Stuffed Bell Peppers
- Creole eggplant Casserole
- Red Beans and Rice (Vegetarian Version)
- Okra and Tomatoes

Breads:

- New Orleans-Style French Bread
- Cajun Cornbread
- Sweet Potato Biscuits
- King Cake

Sauces and Condiments:

- Remoulade Sauce
- Cajun Spice Mix
- Creole Mustard Sauce
- Hot Pepper Jelly
- Blackened Seasoning

Desserts:

- Bananas Foster
- Beignets
- Bread Pudding with Whiskey Sauce
- Pralines
- Pecan Pie with Bourbon
- King Cake Cheesecake
- Creole Cream Cheese Ice Cream
- Sweet Potato Pie
- Cajun Apple Dumplings
- Bourbon Street Chocolate Pecan Pie

Appetizers:

Cajun Shrimp and Grits

Ingredients:

For the Shrimp:

- 1 pound large shrimp, peeled and deveined
- 2 tablespoons Cajun seasoning
- 2 tablespoons olive oil
- 3 cloves garlic, minced
- 1 tablespoon lemon juice
- Salt and pepper to taste
- Fresh parsley, chopped (for garnish)

For the Grits:

- 1 cup stone-ground grits
- 4 cups water
- 1 cup milk
- 1/2 cup cheddar cheese, shredded
- 4 tablespoons unsalted butter
- Salt to taste

Instructions:

1. Prepare the Grits:

- In a medium saucepan, bring water and milk to a boil.
- Slowly whisk in the grits, reduce heat to low, and simmer, stirring frequently, until thickened (about 20-25 minutes).
- Stir in the cheddar cheese, butter, and salt. Keep warm.

2. Cook the Shrimp:

- In a bowl, toss the shrimp with Cajun seasoning, making sure they are well-coated.
- Heat olive oil in a large skillet over medium-high heat. Add minced garlic and sauté until fragrant.
- Add the seasoned shrimp to the skillet and cook for 2-3 minutes per side or until they turn pink and opaque.
- Drizzle lemon juice over the shrimp and season with salt and pepper to taste.

3. Serve:

- Spoon a generous portion of cheesy grits onto each plate.
- Top with the Cajun shrimp.
- Garnish with fresh parsley and serve immediately.

Enjoy this flavorful Cajun Shrimp and Grits appetizer that combines the richness of cheesy grits with the bold and spicy kick of Cajun-seasoned shrimp. Perfect for impressing guests or treating yourself to a taste of Louisiana cuisine!

Crab-Stuffed Mushrooms

Ingredients:

For the Stuffed Mushrooms:

- 1 pound large white mushrooms, cleaned and stems removed
- 8 ounces lump crabmeat, picked over for shells
- 1/2 cup cream cheese, softened
- 1/4 cup mayonnaise
- 1/4 cup grated Parmesan cheese
- 2 green onions, finely chopped
- 2 cloves garlic, minced
- 1 teaspoon Worcestershire sauce
- 1 teaspoon Dijon mustard
- Salt and pepper to taste
- Fresh parsley, chopped (for garnish)

For the Topping:

- 1/2 cup breadcrumbs
- 2 tablespoons melted butter
- 1/4 cup grated Parmesan cheese

Instructions:

1. Preheat the Oven:

- Preheat your oven to 375°F (190°C).

2. Prepare the Mushrooms:

- Clean the mushrooms and remove the stems. Set aside.

3. Make the Crab Filling:

- In a bowl, combine the crabmeat, cream cheese, mayonnaise, Parmesan cheese, green onions, garlic, Worcestershire sauce, Dijon mustard, salt, and pepper. Mix until well combined.

4. Stuff the Mushrooms:

- Spoon the crab filling into each mushroom cap, pressing it down slightly.

5. Prepare the Topping:

- In a small bowl, combine breadcrumbs, melted butter, and Parmesan cheese to create the topping.

6. Bake:

- Place the stuffed mushrooms on a baking sheet.
- Sprinkle the breadcrumb topping over each stuffed mushroom.
- Bake in the preheated oven for 15-20 minutes or until the mushrooms are tender and the topping is golden brown.

7. Serve:

- Garnish with chopped fresh parsley and serve hot.

These Crab-Stuffed Mushrooms make for an elegant and delicious appetizer, perfect for parties or special occasions. The creamy crab filling combined with the crunchy breadcrumb topping creates a delightful bite-sized treat that will impress your guests. Enjoy!

Creole Deviled Eggs

Ingredients:

For the Deviled Eggs:

- 6 large eggs, hard-boiled and peeled
- 1/4 cup mayonnaise
- 1 tablespoon Creole or Dijon mustard
- 1 tablespoon sweet pickle relish
- 1 teaspoon hot sauce (adjust to taste)
- 1/2 teaspoon Worcestershire sauce
- Salt and pepper to taste

For Garnish:

- Paprika
- Fresh chives, chopped

Instructions:

1. Hard-Boil the Eggs:

- Place the eggs in a saucepan and cover them with water.
- Bring the water to a boil, then reduce heat to a simmer and cook for 10-12 minutes.
- Transfer the eggs to an ice water bath to cool, then peel and cut them in half lengthwise.

2. Prepare the Filling:

- Carefully remove the yolks from the halved eggs and place them in a bowl.
- Mash the yolks with a fork and add mayonnaise, Creole or Dijon mustard, sweet pickle relish, hot sauce, Worcestershire sauce, salt, and pepper. Mix until smooth and well combined.

3. Fill the Egg Whites:

- Spoon or pipe the yolk mixture back into the egg whites, creating a smooth and even filling.

4. Garnish:

- Sprinkle a pinch of paprika over each deviled egg for color and a hint of smokiness.
- Garnish with chopped fresh chives.

5. Chill and Serve:

- Refrigerate the deviled eggs for at least 30 minutes before serving to allow the flavors to meld.
- Serve chilled and enjoy!

These Creole Deviled Eggs add a zesty kick to the classic appetizer, making them a perfect addition to any gathering or brunch. The combination of Creole mustard, hot sauce, and Worcestershire sauce adds a flavorful twist that will delight your taste buds.

Crawfish Étouffée Stuffed Jalapeños

Ingredients:

For the Crawfish Étouffée:

- 1 pound crawfish tails, peeled and deveined
- 1/2 cup butter
- 1/2 cup all-purpose flour
- 1 large onion, finely chopped
- 1 bell pepper, finely chopped
- 2 celery stalks, finely chopped
- 3 cloves garlic, minced
- 2 cups chicken or seafood broth
- 1 can (14 ounces) diced tomatoes, undrained
- 1 tablespoon Creole seasoning
- 1 teaspoon Worcestershire sauce
- Salt and pepper to taste
- Green onions, chopped (for garnish)
- Fresh parsley, chopped (for garnish)

For the Stuffed Jalapeños:

- 12 large jalapeños, halved and seeds removed
- 1 cup shredded Monterey Jack cheese
- Crawfish Étouffée mixture

Instructions:

1. Prepare the Crawfish Étouffée:

- In a large skillet, melt the butter over medium heat. Add the flour and stir continuously to make a roux, cooking until it turns a golden brown color.
- Add the chopped onion, bell pepper, celery, and minced garlic. Cook until the vegetables are softened.
- Stir in the crawfish tails and cook for 2-3 minutes.

- Pour in the chicken or seafood broth, diced tomatoes, Creole seasoning, Worcestershire sauce, salt, and pepper. Simmer for 15-20 minutes, allowing the flavors to meld.
- Garnish with chopped green onions and fresh parsley.

2. Prepare the Stuffed Jalapeños:

- Preheat your oven to 375°F (190°C).
- Spoon the Crawfish Étouffée mixture into each halved and deseeded jalapeño.
- Place the stuffed jalapeños on a baking sheet.

3. Bake:

- Sprinkle shredded Monterey Jack cheese over each stuffed jalapeño.
- Bake in the preheated oven for 15-20 minutes or until the cheese is melted and bubbly.

4. Garnish and Serve:

- Remove from the oven and garnish with additional chopped green onions and parsley.
- Serve the Crawfish Étouffée Stuffed Jalapeños as a flavorful and spicy appetizer.

These stuffed jalapeños offer a delightful combination of spice and the rich flavors of Crawfish Étouffée, making them a unique and tasty addition to your Cajun and Creole-inspired menu. Enjoy the bold and zesty kick with every bite!

Boudin Balls with Remoulade Sauce

Ingredients:

For the Boudin Balls:

- 1 pound boudin sausage, casing removed
- 1 cup seasoned breadcrumbs
- 2 large eggs, beaten
- Vegetable oil (for frying)
- Green onions, chopped (for garnish)

For the Remoulade Sauce:

- 1 cup mayonnaise
- 2 tablespoons Creole mustard
- 1 tablespoon hot sauce
- 1 tablespoon Worcestershire sauce
- 2 cloves garlic, minced
- 2 tablespoons capers, chopped
- 2 tablespoons fresh parsley, chopped
- Salt and pepper to taste

Instructions:

1. Prepare the Remoulade Sauce:

- In a bowl, combine mayonnaise, Creole mustard, hot sauce, Worcestershire sauce, minced garlic, capers, chopped fresh parsley, salt, and pepper. Mix well.
- Refrigerate the Remoulade Sauce for at least 30 minutes to allow the flavors to meld.

2. Make the Boudin Balls:

- Take a portion of boudin sausage and shape it into a small ball.
- Roll each boudin ball in the beaten eggs and then coat it with seasoned breadcrumbs. Repeat for all boudin balls.

3. Fry the Boudin Balls:

- Heat vegetable oil in a deep fryer or a large, deep skillet to 350°F (175°C).
- Carefully place the boudin balls into the hot oil and fry until they are golden brown and crispy.
- Use a slotted spoon to remove the boudin balls from the oil and place them on a paper towel-lined plate to drain excess oil.

4. Serve:

- Arrange the Boudin Balls on a serving platter.
- Sprinkle chopped green onions over the top.
- Serve the Boudin Balls hot with the chilled Remoulade Sauce for dipping.

These Boudin Balls with Remoulade Sauce make for a flavorful and satisfying appetizer. The crispy exterior gives way to a savory boudin filling, and the tangy Remoulade Sauce adds a delightful kick. Perfect for gatherings or as a unique addition to your Cajun and Creole-inspired menu!

Andouille Sausage Sliders with Creole Mustard

Ingredients:

For the Andouille Sausage Sliders:

- 1 pound Andouille sausage, sliced into rounds
- Slider buns
- 1 cup coleslaw mix (cabbage and carrots)
- 1 tablespoon olive oil
- Salt and pepper to taste

For the Creole Mustard:

- 1/2 cup Dijon mustard
- 2 tablespoons Creole mustard
- 1 tablespoon honey
- 1 teaspoon hot sauce
- 1 clove garlic, minced
- Salt and pepper to taste

Instructions:

1. Make the Creole Mustard:

- In a small bowl, whisk together Dijon mustard, Creole mustard, honey, hot sauce, minced garlic, salt, and pepper. Adjust the seasoning to taste.
- Refrigerate the Creole Mustard for at least 30 minutes before serving to allow the flavors to meld.

2. Cook the Andouille Sausage:

- Heat olive oil in a skillet over medium-high heat.
- Add Andouille sausage rounds and cook until browned and cooked through, about 3-4 minutes per side.
- Season with salt and pepper to taste.

3. Toast the Slider Buns:

- Lightly toast the slider buns in the skillet or oven.

4. Assemble the Sliders:

   - Place a spoonful of coleslaw mix on the bottom half of each slider bun.
   - Top with a few slices of cooked Andouille sausage.

5. Add Creole Mustard:

   - Drizzle Creole Mustard over the Andouille sausage.
   - Place the top half of the slider bun to complete the sliders.

6. Serve:

   - Arrange the Andouille Sausage Sliders on a serving platter.
   - Serve immediately, and enjoy these zesty sliders with a touch of Creole flavor!

These Andouille Sausage Sliders with Creole Mustard offer a perfect blend of spice and savory goodness. The smoky Andouille sausage pairs well with the tangy and flavorful Creole Mustard, creating a delicious bite-sized treat that's ideal for parties or game day gatherings.

Soups and Gumbos:

Chicken and Sausage Gumbo

Ingredients:

For the Gumbo:

- 1/2 cup vegetable oil
- 1/2 cup all-purpose flour (for roux)
- 1 large onion, finely chopped
- 1 bell pepper, finely chopped
- 2 celery stalks, finely chopped
- 3 cloves garlic, minced
- 1 pound Andouille sausage, sliced
- 4 boneless, skinless chicken thighs, cut into bite-sized pieces
- 1 teaspoon dried thyme
- 1 teaspoon dried oregano
- 1 teaspoon smoked paprika
- 1/2 teaspoon cayenne pepper (adjust to taste)
- 1 bay leaf
- Salt and black pepper to taste
- 6 cups chicken broth
- 1 can (14 ounces) diced tomatoes, undrained
- 1 cup okra, sliced (fresh or frozen)
- 1 cup frozen sliced okra
- 2 cups cooked white rice (for serving)
- Chopped green onions (for garnish)
- Chopped fresh parsley (for garnish)
- File powder (optional, for serving)

Instructions:

1. Make the Roux:

- In a large, heavy-bottomed pot, heat vegetable oil over medium heat.
- Gradually whisk in the flour to create a roux. Cook, stirring constantly, until the roux turns a dark brown color (about 15-20 minutes). Be careful not to burn it.

2. Sauté Vegetables and Meat:

   - Add chopped onions, bell pepper, celery, and minced garlic to the roux. Cook until the vegetables are softened.
   - Stir in sliced Andouille sausage and cook for 5 minutes.
   - Add chicken pieces and cook until they are browned.

3. Season the Gumbo:

   - Season the mixture with dried thyme, dried oregano, smoked paprika, cayenne pepper, bay leaf, salt, and black pepper. Mix well.

4. Add Broth and Tomatoes:

   - Gradually pour in the chicken broth while continuously stirring to avoid lumps.
   - Add diced tomatoes with their juice. Bring the mixture to a boil.

5. Simmer:

   - Reduce the heat to low, cover the pot, and let the gumbo simmer for at least 1 hour, stirring occasionally.

6. Add Okra:

   - Add sliced okra to the gumbo and simmer for an additional 30 minutes.

7. Serve:

   - Remove the bay leaf.
   - Serve the Chicken and Sausage Gumbo over a bed of cooked white rice.
   - Garnish with chopped green onions, fresh parsley, and a sprinkle of file powder if desired.

This hearty and flavorful Chicken and Sausage Gumbo is a classic Cajun dish that will transport you to the heart of Louisiana. Serve it over rice for a complete and satisfying meal. Enjoy the rich blend of spices and textures that make gumbo a beloved dish!

Seafood Okra Gumbo

Ingredients:

For the Gumbo:

- 1/2 cup vegetable oil
- 1/2 cup all-purpose flour (for roux)
- 1 large onion, finely chopped
- 1 bell pepper, finely chopped
- 2 celery stalks, finely chopped
- 3 cloves garlic, minced
- 1 pound okra, sliced (fresh or frozen)
- 1 pound Andouille sausage, sliced
- 1 pound shrimp, peeled and deveined
- 1 pound crab meat (claw or lump)
- 1 teaspoon dried thyme
- 1 teaspoon dried oregano
- 1 teaspoon smoked paprika
- 1/2 teaspoon cayenne pepper (adjust to taste)
- 1 bay leaf
- Salt and black pepper to taste
- 8 cups seafood or chicken broth
- 1 can (14 ounces) diced tomatoes, undrained
- File powder (optional, for serving)
- Cooked white rice (for serving)
- Chopped green onions (for garnish)
- Chopped fresh parsley (for garnish)

Instructions:

1. Make the Roux:

- In a large, heavy-bottomed pot, heat vegetable oil over medium heat.
- Gradually whisk in the flour to create a roux. Cook, stirring constantly, until the roux turns a dark brown color (about 15-20 minutes). Be careful not to burn it.

2. Sauté Vegetables and Meat:

- Add chopped onions, bell pepper, celery, and minced garlic to the roux. Cook until the vegetables are softened.
- Stir in sliced okra and cook for 5 minutes.
- Add sliced Andouille sausage and cook for an additional 5 minutes.
- Add shrimp and crab meat to the pot. Cook until the shrimp are pink and the crab meat is heated through.

3. Season the Gumbo:

- Season the mixture with dried thyme, dried oregano, smoked paprika, cayenne pepper, bay leaf, salt, and black pepper. Mix well.

4. Add Broth and Tomatoes:

- Gradually pour in the seafood or chicken broth while continuously stirring to avoid lumps.
- Add diced tomatoes with their juice. Bring the mixture to a boil.

5. Simmer:

- Reduce the heat to low, cover the pot, and let the gumbo simmer for at least 1 hour, stirring occasionally.

6. Serve:

- Remove the bay leaf.
- Serve the Seafood Okra Gumbo over a bed of cooked white rice.
- Garnish with chopped green onions, fresh parsley, and a sprinkle of file powder if desired.

This Seafood Okra Gumbo is a delicious and hearty dish that celebrates the rich flavors of the Gulf Coast. The combination of shrimp, crab, and Andouille sausage creates a delightful seafood medley in a flavorful roux-based broth. Serve it over rice for a complete Cajun culinary experience!

Shrimp and Corn Bisque

Ingredients:

- 1 pound shrimp, peeled and deveined, shells reserved
- 4 cups fresh or frozen corn kernels
- 4 cups chicken broth
- 1 cup heavy cream
- 1/2 cup unsalted butter
- 1 large onion, finely chopped
- 2 celery stalks, finely chopped
- 1 red bell pepper, finely chopped
- 3 cloves garlic, minced
- 1/4 cup all-purpose flour
- 1 teaspoon smoked paprika
- 1/2 teaspoon cayenne pepper (adjust to taste)
- Salt and black pepper to taste
- 1 bay leaf
- 1 tablespoon fresh thyme leaves
- 1 cup whole milk
- Chopped green onions (for garnish)
- Chopped fresh parsley (for garnish)

Instructions:

1. Prepare Shrimp Stock:

- In a saucepan, combine shrimp shells and chicken broth. Bring to a simmer and let it cook for 15-20 minutes. Strain the stock, discarding the shells, and set aside.

2. Cook the Shrimp:

- In a separate pot, melt 2 tablespoons of butter over medium heat.
- Add shrimp and cook until they turn pink, about 2-3 minutes per side. Remove shrimp from the pot and set aside.

3. Sauté Vegetables:

   - In the same pot, add the remaining butter and sauté onions, celery, red bell pepper, and garlic until softened.

4. Make the Roux:

   - Stir in flour, smoked paprika, and cayenne pepper to create a roux. Cook for 3-4 minutes, stirring constantly.

5. Add Ingredients:

   - Gradually whisk in the strained shrimp stock, chicken broth, and corn kernels.
   - Add bay leaf, thyme, salt, and black pepper. Bring the mixture to a simmer.

6. Blend and Simmer:

   - Use an immersion blender to partially blend the bisque, leaving some chunks for texture.
   - Stir in heavy cream and milk. Simmer for an additional 10-15 minutes.

7. Add Shrimp:

   - Dice the cooked shrimp and add them to the bisque. Cook for an additional 5 minutes until the shrimp are heated through.

8. Adjust Seasoning and Serve:

   - Adjust salt, pepper, and spice levels to taste.
   - Discard the bay leaf and serve the Shrimp and Corn Bisque hot.
   - Garnish with chopped green onions and fresh parsley.

This Shrimp and Corn Bisque is a velvety and flavorful soup that combines the sweetness of corn with the rich taste of shrimp. Perfect for warming up on a chilly day, this bisque is sure to become a comforting favorite.

Creole Chicken and Sausage Soup

Ingredients:

- 1 pound boneless, skinless chicken thighs, cut into bite-sized pieces
- 1/2 pound Andouille sausage, sliced
- 1 large onion, finely chopped
- 1 bell pepper, finely chopped
- 2 celery stalks, finely chopped
- 3 cloves garlic, minced
- 1 can (14 ounces) diced tomatoes, undrained
- 1 cup okra, sliced (fresh or frozen)
- 6 cups chicken broth
- 1 teaspoon dried thyme
- 1 teaspoon dried oregano
- 1 teaspoon smoked paprika
- 1/2 teaspoon cayenne pepper (adjust to taste)
- 2 bay leaves
- Salt and black pepper to taste
- 1 cup white rice, cooked (for serving)
- Chopped green onions (for garnish)
- Chopped fresh parsley (for garnish)

Instructions:

1. Sauté Chicken and Sausage:

- In a large pot, brown the chicken pieces and Andouille sausage over medium-high heat until the chicken is no longer pink. Remove and set aside.

2. Sauté Vegetables:

- In the same pot, sauté onions, bell pepper, celery, and minced garlic until the vegetables are softened.

3. Add Tomatoes and Spices:

- Stir in diced tomatoes, dried thyme, dried oregano, smoked paprika, cayenne pepper, bay leaves, salt, and black pepper.

4. Incorporate Chicken and Sausage:

- Return the browned chicken and Andouille sausage to the pot. Mix well.

5. Add Broth and Okra:

- Pour in chicken broth and add sliced okra. Bring the mixture to a simmer.

6. Simmer:

- Cover the pot and let the soup simmer for at least 30 minutes, allowing the flavors to meld. Stir occasionally.

7. Adjust Seasoning and Serve:

- Taste the soup and adjust the seasoning as needed.
- Remove the bay leaves.
- Serve the Creole Chicken and Sausage Soup over a scoop of cooked white rice.
- Garnish with chopped green onions and fresh parsley.

This Creole Chicken and Sausage Soup is a comforting and hearty dish that brings the vibrant flavors of the Louisiana bayou to your table. With a perfect blend of chicken, Andouille sausage, and traditional Creole spices, this soup is sure to warm you up on a chilly day. Enjoy the delicious combination of savory and spicy notes!

Red Beans and Rice Soup

Ingredients:

- 1 cup dried red kidney beans, soaked overnight and drained
- 1 tablespoon vegetable oil
- 1 large onion, finely chopped
- 1 bell pepper, finely chopped
- 2 celery stalks, finely chopped
- 3 cloves garlic, minced
- 1 pound Andouille sausage, sliced
- 1 teaspoon dried thyme
- 1 teaspoon dried oregano
- 1 teaspoon smoked paprika
- 1/2 teaspoon cayenne pepper (adjust to taste)
- 6 cups chicken broth
- 1 can (14 ounces) diced tomatoes, undrained
- Salt and black pepper to taste
- 2 bay leaves
- 1 cup long-grain white rice, cooked
- Chopped green onions (for garnish)
- Chopped fresh parsley (for garnish)

Instructions:

1. Cook the Red Beans:

- In a large pot, combine soaked red kidney beans with enough water to cover them. Bring to a boil, then reduce heat and simmer for about 45-60 minutes, or until beans are tender. Drain and set aside.

2. Sauté Vegetables and Sausage:

- In the same pot, heat vegetable oil over medium-high heat. Sauté onions, bell pepper, celery, and minced garlic until vegetables are softened.
- Add Andouille sausage slices and cook until browned.

3. Add Spices and Tomatoes:

   - Stir in dried thyme, dried oregano, smoked paprika, and cayenne pepper. Add diced tomatoes with their juice. Mix well.

4. Incorporate Red Beans and Broth:

   - Return the cooked red kidney beans to the pot. Pour in chicken broth and add bay leaves. Bring the mixture to a simmer.

5. Simmer:

   - Cover the pot and let the soup simmer for at least 30 minutes, allowing the flavors to meld. Stir occasionally.

6. Adjust Seasoning and Serve:

   - Taste the soup and adjust the seasoning with salt, black pepper, and additional cayenne pepper if desired.
   - Remove the bay leaves.
   - Serve the Red Beans and Rice Soup over a scoop of cooked white rice.
   - Garnish with chopped green onions and fresh parsley.

This Red Beans and Rice Soup offers a twist on the classic Louisiana dish, providing all the flavors of red beans and rice in a comforting soup form. The combination of red kidney beans, Andouille sausage, and traditional Creole spices creates a flavorful and satisfying meal. Enjoy the hearty goodness of this Southern-inspired soup!

Oyster and Artichoke Soup

Ingredients:

- 2 dozen fresh oysters, shucked, with their liquor
- 2 tablespoons unsalted butter
- 1 large onion, finely chopped
- 2 celery stalks, finely chopped
- 2 cloves garlic, minced
- 1 can (14 ounces) artichoke hearts, drained and chopped
- 4 cups chicken broth
- 1 cup heavy cream
- 1/4 cup all-purpose flour
- 1/2 cup dry white wine
- 1 teaspoon dried thyme
- 1 teaspoon Old Bay seasoning
- Salt and black pepper to taste
- 2 tablespoons fresh parsley, chopped (for garnish)
- Lemon wedges (for serving)

Instructions:

1. Prepare Oysters:

   - Shuck the oysters, reserving their liquor. Set aside.

2. Sauté Vegetables:

   - In a large pot, melt the butter over medium heat. Add chopped onions, celery, and minced garlic. Sauté until the vegetables are softened.

3. Add Artichokes:

   - Stir in chopped artichoke hearts and cook for an additional 2-3 minutes.

4. Make Roux:

   - Sprinkle flour over the vegetable mixture and stir to create a roux. Cook for 2-3 minutes, stirring constantly.

5. Incorporate Broth and Liquor:

- Gradually pour in chicken broth, oyster liquor, and dry white wine. Mix well to avoid lumps.

6. Add Seasonings:

- Season the soup with dried thyme, Old Bay seasoning, salt, and black pepper. Bring the mixture to a simmer.

7. Cook Oysters:

- Gently add the shucked oysters to the simmering soup. Cook just until the oysters are plump and the edges begin to curl, about 2-3 minutes.

8. Finish with Cream:

- Pour in the heavy cream, stirring gently. Heat through but do not boil to prevent curdling.

9. Adjust Seasoning and Serve:

- Taste the soup and adjust the seasoning if needed.
- Ladle the Oyster and Artichoke Soup into bowls.
- Garnish with chopped fresh parsley.
- Serve hot with lemon wedges on the side.

This Oyster and Artichoke Soup is a rich and elegant dish that brings together the briny goodness of fresh oysters with the earthy flavor of artichokes. The velvety texture and delicate balance of flavors make it a delightful choice for a special occasion or a luxurious meal. Enjoy the unique combination of ingredients in this decadent seafood soup!

Main Dishes - Seafood:

Blackened Catfish

Ingredients:

- 4 catfish fillets
- 1/2 cup unsalted butter, melted
- 2 tablespoons paprika
- 1 tablespoon onion powder
- 1 tablespoon garlic powder
- 1 teaspoon dried thyme
- 1 teaspoon dried oregano
- 1 teaspoon cayenne pepper (adjust to taste)
- 1 teaspoon black pepper
- 1 teaspoon white pepper
- 1 teaspoon salt
- Lemon wedges (for serving)

Instructions:

1. Preheat the Cast Iron Skillet:

- Place a cast-iron skillet over high heat and preheat until it is very hot.

2. Prepare the Blackening Seasoning:

- In a small bowl, mix together paprika, onion powder, garlic powder, dried thyme, dried oregano, cayenne pepper, black pepper, white pepper, and salt.

3. Coat the Catfish:

- Pat the catfish fillets dry with paper towels.
- Brush each fillet with melted butter, ensuring they are well-coated on both sides.

4. Apply the Blackening Seasoning:

- Generously sprinkle the blackening seasoning over each side of the catfish fillets, pressing the seasoning into the fish to adhere.

5. Blacken the Catfish:

- Carefully place the seasoned catfish fillets in the hot cast-iron skillet.
- Cook for 3-4 minutes on each side or until the fish is blackened and cooked through. The high heat is essential to create the blackened crust.

6. Rest and Serve:

- Remove the catfish fillets from the skillet and let them rest for a couple of minutes.
- Serve hot with lemon wedges on the side for squeezing.

7. Optional Oven Finish (for thicker fillets):

- If using thicker catfish fillets, after blackening both sides in the skillet, you can finish cooking them in a preheated oven at 375°F (190°C) for an additional 5-7 minutes until they reach the desired doneness.

8. Serve and Enjoy:

- Plate the Blackened Catfish and serve immediately.
- Enjoy the spicy, flavorful crust and tender catfish!

This Blackened Catfish recipe offers a bold and spicy flavor with a crispy exterior and moist, tender inside. Serve it with your favorite sides like rice, vegetables, or a refreshing salad for a complete and satisfying meal.

Jambalaya with Shrimp, Chicken, and Andouille Sausage

Ingredients:

- 1 pound large shrimp, peeled and deveined
- 1 pound boneless, skinless chicken thighs, cut into bite-sized pieces
- 1/2 pound Andouille sausage, sliced
- 2 tablespoons vegetable oil
- 1 large onion, finely chopped
- 1 bell pepper, finely chopped
- 2 celery stalks, finely chopped
- 3 cloves garlic, minced
- 1 can (14 ounces) diced tomatoes, undrained
- 2 cups long-grain white rice
- 4 cups chicken broth
- 2 teaspoons Cajun seasoning
- 1 teaspoon dried thyme
- 1 teaspoon dried oregano
- 1 teaspoon smoked paprika
- 1/2 teaspoon cayenne pepper (adjust to taste)
- Salt and black pepper to taste
- 2 bay leaves
- Chopped green onions (for garnish)
- Chopped fresh parsley (for garnish)

Instructions:

1. Season and Brown Meat:

- In a large pot or Dutch oven, heat vegetable oil over medium-high heat.
- Season the chicken pieces and shrimp with Cajun seasoning, salt, and black pepper.
- Brown the chicken pieces in the pot, then add the Andouille sausage and cook until browned.
- Add the shrimp and cook until they just turn pink. Remove the meat and shrimp from the pot and set aside.

2. Sauté Vegetables:

- In the same pot, add more oil if needed. Sauté onions, bell pepper, celery, and garlic until the vegetables are softened.

3. Add Tomatoes and Spices:

- Stir in diced tomatoes with their juice. Add dried thyme, dried oregano, smoked paprika, and cayenne pepper. Mix well.

4. Add Rice and Broth:

- Add the rice to the pot and cook, stirring frequently, until the rice is lightly toasted.
- Pour in chicken broth and add bay leaves. Bring the mixture to a boil.

5. Combine Meat and Shrimp:

- Return the browned chicken, Andouille sausage, and shrimp to the pot. Mix everything well.

6. Simmer:

- Reduce the heat to low, cover the pot, and let the Jambalaya simmer for about 20-25 minutes or until the rice is cooked and has absorbed the liquid.

7. Adjust Seasoning and Serve:

- Taste the Jambalaya and adjust the seasoning with salt, black pepper, and Cajun seasoning if needed.
- Remove the bay leaves.
- Serve the Jambalaya hot, garnished with chopped green onions and fresh parsley.

This Jambalaya with Shrimp, Chicken, and Andouille Sausage is a flavorful and hearty one-pot dish that captures the essence of Cajun and Creole cuisine. With a perfect blend of spices, meats, and rice, it's a delicious celebration of Louisiana flavors. Enjoy this classic comfort food with a touch of Southern charm!

Shrimp Creole

Ingredients:

- 1 pound large shrimp, peeled and deveined
- 2 tablespoons vegetable oil
- 1 large onion, finely chopped
- 1 bell pepper, finely chopped
- 2 celery stalks, finely chopped
- 3 cloves garlic, minced
- 1 can (14 ounces) crushed tomatoes
- 1 can (8 ounces) tomato sauce
- 1 cup chicken broth
- 1 teaspoon sugar
- 1 teaspoon Worcestershire sauce
- 1 teaspoon hot sauce (adjust to taste)
- 1 teaspoon dried thyme
- 1 teaspoon dried oregano
- 1 bay leaf
- Salt and black pepper to taste
- Cooked white rice (for serving)
- Chopped green onions (for garnish)
- Chopped fresh parsley (for garnish)

Instructions:

1. Sauté Vegetables:

- In a large skillet or Dutch oven, heat vegetable oil over medium heat. Sauté onions, bell pepper, celery, and garlic until the vegetables are softened.

2. Add Tomatoes and Sauce:

- Stir in crushed tomatoes, tomato sauce, and chicken broth.

3. Season:

- Add sugar, Worcestershire sauce, hot sauce, dried thyme, dried oregano, bay leaf, salt, and black pepper. Mix well.

4. Simmer:

- Bring the mixture to a simmer, then reduce the heat to low. Cover and let it simmer for about 15-20 minutes to allow the flavors to meld.

5. Cook Shrimp:

- Add the peeled and deveined shrimp to the simmering sauce. Cook for 3-5 minutes or until the shrimp turn pink and opaque.

6. Adjust Seasoning:

- Taste the Shrimp Creole and adjust the seasoning with salt, black pepper, and hot sauce if needed.

7. Serve:

- Remove the bay leaf.
- Serve the Shrimp Creole over a bed of cooked white rice.
- Garnish with chopped green onions and fresh parsley.

This Shrimp Creole is a classic Louisiana dish that showcases the vibrant flavors of the Gulf Coast. The combination of tomatoes, spices, and succulent shrimp creates a savory and satisfying meal. Serve it over rice for a complete and comforting experience that brings the taste of New Orleans to your table!

Crawfish Pie

Ingredients:

For the Pie Crust:

- 2 1/2 cups all-purpose flour
- 1 cup unsalted butter, chilled and cubed
- 1/4 cup ice water
- 1 teaspoon salt

For the Crawfish Filling:

- 1 pound crawfish tail meat, peeled and deveined
- 1/2 cup unsalted butter
- 1 cup onion, finely chopped
- 1/2 cup bell pepper, finely chopped
- 1/2 cup celery, finely chopped
- 2 cloves garlic, minced
- 1/4 cup all-purpose flour
- 1 cup chicken or seafood broth
- 1/2 cup heavy cream
- 1 tablespoon tomato paste
- 1 teaspoon Cajun seasoning
- Salt and black pepper to taste
- 1/4 cup green onions, chopped
- 1/4 cup fresh parsley, chopped

Instructions:

1. Prepare the Pie Crust:

- In a food processor, combine flour and salt. Add chilled and cubed butter. Pulse until the mixture resembles coarse crumbs.
- Gradually add ice water and pulse until the dough comes together.
- Divide the dough into two discs, wrap in plastic wrap, and refrigerate for at least 1 hour.

2. Make the Crawfish Filling:

- In a large skillet, melt butter over medium heat. Add chopped onions, bell pepper, celery, and garlic. Cook until the vegetables are softened.
- Stir in flour to create a roux. Cook for 2-3 minutes, stirring constantly.
- Gradually add chicken or seafood broth, heavy cream, tomato paste, Cajun seasoning, salt, and black pepper. Cook until the mixture thickens.
- Add crawfish tail meat, green onions, and fresh parsley. Simmer for an additional 5 minutes. Adjust seasoning to taste.

3. Roll out the Pie Crust:

- Preheat oven to 375°F (190°C).
- Roll out one disc of the chilled pie crust on a floured surface to fit a pie dish. Place the rolled-out crust in the pie dish.

4. Assemble and Bake:

- Pour the crawfish filling into the pie crust.
- Roll out the second disc of pie crust and place it over the filling. Trim excess crust and crimp the edges to seal.
- Cut a few slits in the top crust to allow steam to escape.
- Bake for 30-35 minutes or until the crust is golden brown.

5. Serve:

- Allow the Crawfish Pie to cool for a few minutes before slicing.
- Serve warm and enjoy this flavorful Louisiana classic!

This Crawfish Pie is a savory delight that captures the essence of Cajun and Creole cuisine. With a buttery and flaky crust and a rich crawfish filling, it's a perfect dish to celebrate the unique flavors of the Gulf Coast. Enjoy a slice of this savory pie for a taste of Louisiana in every bite!

Cajun Grilled Lobster Tails

Ingredients:

- 4 lobster tails, split in half lengthwise
- 1/2 cup unsalted butter, melted
- 2 tablespoons olive oil
- 2 teaspoons Cajun seasoning
- 1 teaspoon paprika
- 1 teaspoon garlic powder
- 1 teaspoon onion powder
- 1/2 teaspoon dried thyme
- 1/2 teaspoon dried oregano
- 1/2 teaspoon cayenne pepper (adjust to taste)
- Salt and black pepper to taste
- Fresh lemon wedges (for serving)
- Chopped fresh parsley (for garnish)

Instructions:

1. Preheat the Grill:

- Preheat your grill to medium-high heat.

2. Prepare the Lobster Tails:

- Use kitchen shears to cut through the top shell of the lobster tails, stopping at the tail. Gently spread the shell open, exposing the lobster meat.

3. Cajun Butter Mixture:

- In a bowl, combine melted butter, olive oil, Cajun seasoning, paprika, garlic powder, onion powder, dried thyme, dried oregano, cayenne pepper, salt, and black pepper. Mix well to create the Cajun butter mixture.

4. Brush with Cajun Butter:

- Brush the Cajun butter mixture generously over the exposed lobster meat.

5. Grill the Lobster Tails:

- Place the lobster tails on the preheated grill, meat side down. Grill for 4-5 minutes.
- Flip the lobster tails, shell side down, and continue grilling for another 4-5 minutes or until the lobster meat is opaque and cooked through. Baste with additional Cajun butter during grilling.

6. Serve:

- Remove the grilled lobster tails from the grill and transfer them to a serving platter.
- Drizzle any remaining Cajun butter over the lobster tails.
- Garnish with chopped fresh parsley and serve with lemon wedges on the side.

7. Enjoy:

- Serve these Cajun Grilled Lobster Tails immediately and savor the flavorful and spicy goodness with a squeeze of fresh lemon.

This Cajun Grilled Lobster Tails recipe adds a spicy kick to the succulent lobster meat, creating a delightful dish that's perfect for a special occasion or a backyard barbecue. The Cajun butter infusion adds layers of flavor, making each bite a taste of Louisiana's vibrant culinary heritage. Enjoy the bold and delicious experience!

Creole Crab Cakes

Ingredients:

- 1 pound lump crab meat, picked over for shells
- 1/2 cup mayonnaise
- 1 large egg
- 1 tablespoon Dijon mustard
- 1 tablespoon Worcestershire sauce
- 1 tablespoon hot sauce (adjust to taste)
- 1/2 cup finely chopped green onions
- 1/4 cup finely chopped celery
- 1/4 cup finely chopped red bell pepper
- 1/4 cup fresh parsley, finely chopped
- 1 1/2 cups breadcrumbs (divided)
- 1 teaspoon Creole seasoning (store-bought or homemade)
- Salt and black pepper to taste
- Vegetable oil for frying
- Lemon wedges (for serving)
- Creole Remoulade Sauce (for serving, optional)

Instructions:

1. Prepare Crab Cake Mixture:

- In a large bowl, gently combine lump crab meat, mayonnaise, egg, Dijon mustard, Worcestershire sauce, hot sauce, green onions, celery, red bell pepper, parsley, 1/2 cup breadcrumbs, Creole seasoning, salt, and black pepper. Be careful not to break up the crab meat too much.

2. Shape Crab Cakes:

- Divide the crab mixture into equal portions and shape them into crab cakes. Place the remaining breadcrumbs on a plate and coat each crab cake with breadcrumbs, pressing lightly to adhere.

3. Chill:

- Place the crab cakes on a baking sheet and refrigerate for at least 30 minutes. This helps the crab cakes hold their shape during cooking.

4. Fry Crab Cakes:

- Heat vegetable oil in a skillet over medium-high heat.
- Fry the crab cakes in batches until they are golden brown on both sides, about 3-4 minutes per side. Be gentle when flipping to avoid breaking them.

5. Drain and Serve:

- Place the fried crab cakes on a paper towel-lined plate to drain excess oil.

6. Serve:

- Serve the Creole Crab Cakes hot, garnished with fresh parsley and lemon wedges on the side.
- Optionally, serve with Creole Remoulade Sauce for dipping.

7. Enjoy:

- Enjoy these Creole Crab Cakes as a flavorful appetizer or main course, relishing the perfect blend of crab and Creole seasonings.

These Creole Crab Cakes are a delicious fusion of flavors, combining the sweetness of lump crab meat with the zesty kick of Creole seasoning. Serve them as an appetizer at gatherings or as a delightful main course for a special dinner. The crispy exterior and tender crab-filled interior make them a crowd-pleaser!

Main Dishes - Poultry:

Chicken and Andouille Sausage Étouffée

Ingredients:

- 1 pound boneless, skinless chicken thighs, cut into bite-sized pieces
- 1/2 pound Andouille sausage, sliced
- 1/2 cup unsalted butter
- 1/2 cup all-purpose flour
- 1 large onion, finely chopped
- 1 bell pepper, finely chopped
- 2 celery stalks, finely chopped
- 3 cloves garlic, minced
- 1 can (14 ounces) diced tomatoes, undrained
- 2 cups chicken broth
- 1 teaspoon dried thyme
- 1 teaspoon dried oregano
- 1 teaspoon smoked paprika
- 1/2 teaspoon cayenne pepper (adjust to taste)
- Salt and black pepper to taste
- 2 bay leaves
- Chopped green onions (for garnish)
- Chopped fresh parsley (for garnish)
- Cooked white rice (for serving)

Instructions:

1. Prepare Roux:

- In a large, heavy-bottomed pot, melt butter over medium heat. Gradually whisk in flour to create a roux. Cook, stirring constantly, until the roux turns a dark brown color, about 15-20 minutes. Be careful not to burn it.

2. Sauté Chicken and Sausage:

- Add chicken pieces and Andouille sausage to the roux. Cook until the chicken is browned and the sausage is cooked through.

3. Sauté Vegetables:

- Add chopped onions, bell pepper, celery, and minced garlic to the pot. Cook until the vegetables are softened.

4. Add Tomatoes and Spices:

- Stir in diced tomatoes with their juice. Season with dried thyme, dried oregano, smoked paprika, cayenne pepper, salt, and black pepper. Mix well.

5. Pour in Broth:

- Gradually pour in chicken broth while stirring to avoid lumps.

6. Simmer:

- Add bay leaves to the pot. Bring the mixture to a boil, then reduce the heat to low. Cover and let it simmer for at least 30 minutes, stirring occasionally.

7. Adjust Seasoning:

- Taste and adjust the seasoning as needed.

8. Serve:

- Remove the bay leaves.
- Serve the Chicken and Andouille Sausage Étouffée over a bed of cooked white rice.
- Garnish with chopped green onions and fresh parsley.

This Chicken and Andouille Sausage Étouffée is a classic Cajun dish that combines the rich flavors of roux, chicken, and Andouille sausage with a medley of aromatic vegetables. Served over rice, this dish provides a hearty and comforting experience that captures the essence of Louisiana cuisine. Enjoy the bold and savory taste of this traditional Étouffée!

Bourbon Street Chicken

Ingredients:

- 1 1/2 pounds boneless, skinless chicken thighs, cut into bite-sized pieces
- 1/4 cup soy sauce
- 1/4 cup bourbon
- 1/4 cup brown sugar
- 2 tablespoons ketchup
- 2 tablespoons apple cider vinegar
- 1 tablespoon olive oil
- 3 cloves garlic, minced
- 1 teaspoon ginger, grated
- 1/2 teaspoon red pepper flakes (adjust to taste)
- 1/4 teaspoon black pepper
- 2 green onions, chopped (for garnish)
- Sesame seeds (for garnish)
- Cooked white rice (for serving)

Instructions:

1. Marinate the Chicken:

   - In a bowl, whisk together soy sauce, bourbon, brown sugar, ketchup, apple cider vinegar, olive oil, minced garlic, grated ginger, red pepper flakes, and black pepper to create the marinade.

2. Marinate Chicken:

   - Place the chicken pieces in a resealable plastic bag or shallow dish. Pour half of the marinade over the chicken, ensuring all pieces are coated. Reserve the other half for later.

3. Refrigerate:

   - Seal the bag or cover the dish and refrigerate for at least 30 minutes to allow the chicken to marinate.

4. Cook the Chicken:

- Heat a skillet or wok over medium-high heat. Remove the chicken from the marinade, allowing excess marinade to drip off.
- Cook the chicken in the skillet until browned and cooked through, about 5-7 minutes.

5. Make the Sauce:

- In a small saucepan, heat the reserved marinade over medium heat. Bring it to a simmer and cook for 5 minutes until it thickens.

6. Combine Sauce and Chicken:

- Pour the thickened sauce over the cooked chicken in the skillet. Toss to coat the chicken evenly with the sauce.

7. Garnish and Serve:

- Serve the Bourbon Street Chicken over a bed of cooked white rice.
- Garnish with chopped green onions and sesame seeds.

8. Enjoy:

- Enjoy this flavorful Bourbon Street Chicken that combines the sweet and savory notes of bourbon and soy sauce. It's a delicious and easy-to-make dish inspired by the vibrant flavors of New Orleans!

This Bourbon Street Chicken recipe offers a taste of the lively and spirited atmosphere of New Orleans. The combination of bourbon, soy sauce, and brown sugar creates a sweet and savory glaze that perfectly complements the tender chicken pieces. Serve it over rice for a complete and satisfying meal!

Creole Roast Chicken

Ingredients:

- 1 whole chicken (about 4-5 pounds), giblets removed
- 1/4 cup olive oil
- 2 tablespoons Creole seasoning
- 1 tablespoon paprika
- 1 tablespoon dried thyme
- 1 tablespoon dried oregano
- 1 teaspoon onion powder
- 1 teaspoon garlic powder
- 1 teaspoon cayenne pepper (adjust to taste)
- Salt and black pepper to taste
- 1 lemon, halved
- 1 onion, quartered
- 4 garlic cloves, peeled
- Fresh thyme and rosemary sprigs (optional, for stuffing)
- 1 cup chicken broth

Instructions:

1. Preheat the Oven:

- Preheat your oven to 425°F (220°C).

2. Prepare the Chicken:

- Pat the whole chicken dry with paper towels. Ensure the cavity is clean, and remove any leftover giblets.

3. Make Creole Spice Rub:

- In a small bowl, mix together Creole seasoning, paprika, dried thyme, dried oregano, onion powder, garlic powder, cayenne pepper, salt, and black pepper.

4. Rub the Chicken:

- Rub the entire chicken, including the cavity, with olive oil. Sprinkle the Creole spice rub evenly over the chicken, massaging it into the skin.

5. Stuff the Chicken:

    - Stuff the cavity with halved lemon, quartered onion, garlic cloves, and optional thyme and rosemary sprigs.

6. Truss the Chicken:

    - If desired, truss the chicken to help it cook evenly. Tie the legs together using kitchen twine.

7. Roast in the Oven:

    - Place the chicken on a roasting rack in a roasting pan. Pour chicken broth into the bottom of the pan.

8. Roast:

    - Roast the chicken in the preheated oven for about 1 hour and 15 minutes or until the internal temperature reaches 165°F (74°C). Baste the chicken with pan juices every 30 minutes for a golden and crispy skin.

9. Rest and Carve:

    - Allow the roasted chicken to rest for about 15 minutes before carving. This helps the juices redistribute.

10. Serve:

    - Carve the Creole Roast Chicken and serve it with the flavorful pan juices.

11. Enjoy:

- Enjoy this Creole-inspired roast chicken with its aromatic spices and tender meat. Serve it with your favorite sides for a delicious and satisfying meal!

This Creole Roast Chicken brings the vibrant flavors of the Louisiana Creole cuisine to a classic roasted chicken. The blend of Creole spices adds a kick to the golden-brown skin, while the lemon and aromatic herbs infuse the meat with incredible flavor. It's a perfect centerpiece for a festive meal or a flavorful family dinner.

Smothered Turkey Wings

Ingredients:

- 4 turkey wings
- Salt and black pepper to taste
- 1 teaspoon garlic powder
- 1 teaspoon onion powder
- 1 teaspoon dried thyme
- 1 teaspoon smoked paprika
- 1/2 teaspoon cayenne pepper (adjust to taste)
- 1/4 cup all-purpose flour
- 1/4 cup vegetable oil
- 1 large onion, thinly sliced
- 1 bell pepper, thinly sliced
- 2 celery stalks, thinly sliced
- 3 cloves garlic, minced
- 1 cup chicken broth
- 1 bay leaf
- Chopped green onions (for garnish)
- Chopped fresh parsley (for garnish)
- Cooked rice (for serving)

Instructions:

1. Prepare Turkey Wings:

   - Rinse the turkey wings and pat them dry with paper towels. Season with salt, black pepper, garlic powder, onion powder, dried thyme, smoked paprika, and cayenne pepper.

2. Dredge in Flour:

   - Dredge the seasoned turkey wings in flour, shaking off excess.

3. Brown the Turkey Wings:

   - In a large, deep skillet or Dutch oven, heat vegetable oil over medium-high heat. Brown the turkey wings on all sides until golden. Remove from the skillet and set aside.

4. Sauté Vegetables:

- In the same skillet, add sliced onions, bell peppers, and celery. Sauté until the vegetables are softened.

5. Make Gravy:

- Stir in minced garlic and cook for an additional minute. Sprinkle any remaining flour over the vegetables and stir to create a roux.
- Slowly whisk in chicken broth, ensuring there are no lumps. Add the bay leaf.

6. Add Turkey Wings:

- Return the browned turkey wings to the skillet, nestling them into the vegetable mixture.

7. Simmer:

- Bring the mixture to a simmer. Cover and let it simmer on low heat for 1.5 to 2 hours or until the turkey wings are tender and cooked through. Stir occasionally.

8. Adjust Seasoning:

- Taste the gravy and adjust the seasoning with salt, black pepper, and cayenne pepper if needed.

9. Garnish and Serve:

- Remove the bay leaf. Garnish with chopped green onions and fresh parsley.
- Serve the Smothered Turkey Wings over cooked rice.

10. Enjoy:

- Enjoy these tender and flavorful Smothered Turkey Wings, immersed in a rich and savory gravy, served over a bed of rice.

This Smothered Turkey Wings recipe provides a comforting and hearty dish with a perfect blend of spices and a savory gravy. The slow simmering of the turkey wings in the flavorful mixture ensures a delicious and satisfying meal that captures the essence of Southern comfort food.

Cajun Stuffed Chicken Breast

Ingredients:

For the Cajun Seasoning:

- 2 teaspoons paprika
- 1 teaspoon onion powder
- 1 teaspoon garlic powder
- 1 teaspoon dried thyme
- 1 teaspoon dried oregano
- 1/2 teaspoon cayenne pepper (adjust to taste)
- 1/2 teaspoon black pepper
- 1/2 teaspoon white pepper
- 1/2 teaspoon smoked paprika
- 1/2 teaspoon dried basil
- 1/2 teaspoon dried parsley
- Salt to taste

For the Stuffed Chicken:

- 4 boneless, skinless chicken breasts
- Cajun seasoning (for seasoning chicken)
- 4 ounces cream cheese, softened
- 1/2 cup cooked andouille sausage, finely diced
- 1/2 cup bell pepper, finely diced
- 1/4 cup green onions, finely chopped
- 2 cloves garlic, minced
- Salt and black pepper to taste
- Olive oil for cooking

Instructions:

1. Make Cajun Seasoning:

    - In a small bowl, combine all Cajun seasoning ingredients. Adjust salt to taste.

2. Butterfly Chicken Breasts:

    - Preheat your oven to 375°F (190°C).

- Butterfly each chicken breast by slicing horizontally, almost but not entirely through, and open like a book.

3. Season Chicken:

    - Season the inside and outside of each chicken breast with Cajun seasoning.

4. Make Stuffing:

    - In a mixing bowl, combine softened cream cheese, diced andouille sausage, bell pepper, green onions, minced garlic, salt, and black pepper.

5. Stuff Chicken Breasts:

    - Spoon the cream cheese mixture onto one side of each butterflied chicken breast. Fold the other side over the stuffing, creating a stuffed chicken breast.

6. Secure with Toothpicks:

    - Use toothpicks to secure the edges of the stuffed chicken breast and keep the filling inside.

7. Sear Chicken:

    - Heat olive oil in an oven-safe skillet over medium-high heat. Sear the stuffed chicken breasts on both sides until browned.

8. Finish in the Oven:

    - Transfer the skillet to the preheated oven and bake for about 20-25 minutes or until the chicken is cooked through.

9. Rest and Serve:

    - Allow the stuffed chicken breasts to rest for a few minutes before slicing.
    - Remove toothpicks before serving.

10. Enjoy:

- Serve the Cajun Stuffed Chicken Breast slices with your favorite sides and savor the flavorful and spicy Cajun-inspired filling.

These Cajun Stuffed Chicken Breasts offer a burst of flavors with the seasoned cream cheese stuffing and the perfectly spiced Cajun seasoning. This dish is not only visually appealing but also a delightful combination of creamy, savory, and spicy elements. Serve it as a show-stopping main course for a special dinner or any occasion that calls for a touch of Cajun flair!

Turkey and Sausage Gumbo

Ingredients:

- 1 cup vegetable oil
- 1 cup all-purpose flour
- 1 large onion, finely chopped
- 1 bell pepper, finely chopped
- 2 celery stalks, finely chopped
- 3 cloves garlic, minced
- 1 pound Andouille sausage, sliced
- 3 cups cooked turkey meat, shredded
- 8 cups turkey or chicken broth
- 1 bay leaf
- 1 teaspoon dried thyme
- 1 teaspoon dried oregano
- 1 teaspoon paprika
- 1/2 teaspoon cayenne pepper (adjust to taste)
- Salt and black pepper to taste
- 1 cup okra, sliced (fresh or frozen)
- 1 cup frozen sliced okra (optional)
- 2 tablespoons gumbo file powder
- Cooked white rice (for serving)
- Chopped green onions (for garnish)
- Chopped fresh parsley (for garnish)

Instructions:

1. Make Roux:

- In a large, heavy pot, combine vegetable oil and flour over medium heat to make a roux. Stir continuously to avoid burning. Cook until the roux reaches a dark chocolate color, about 15-20 minutes.

2. Sauté Vegetables:

- Add chopped onions, bell pepper, celery, and minced garlic to the roux. Cook until the vegetables are softened.

3. Add Andouille Sausage:

- Stir in sliced Andouille sausage and cook for an additional 5 minutes.

4. Incorporate Turkey Meat:

- Add shredded turkey meat to the pot and mix well.

5. Pour Broth:

- Gradually pour in turkey or chicken broth while stirring to avoid lumps.

6. Season:

- Add bay leaf, dried thyme, dried oregano, paprika, cayenne pepper, salt, and black pepper. Stir to combine.

7. Simmer:

- Bring the gumbo to a simmer. Let it cook for about 30 minutes, allowing the flavors to meld.

8. Add Okra:

- Add sliced fresh okra and frozen okra (if using). Simmer for an additional 15-20 minutes.

9. Gumbo File Powder:

- Stir in gumbo file powder to thicken the gumbo.

10. Adjust Seasoning:

- Taste the gumbo and adjust the seasoning with salt, black pepper, and cayenne pepper if needed.

11. Serve:

- Remove the bay leaf.
- Serve the Turkey and Sausage Gumbo over a bed of cooked white rice.

12. Garnish:

- Garnish with chopped green onions and fresh parsley.

13. Enjoy:

- Enjoy this hearty and flavorful Turkey and Sausage Gumbo, a comforting dish with a rich blend of spices and textures.

This Turkey and Sausage Gumbo is a delicious way to use leftover turkey, combining it with Andouille sausage and a flavorful roux-based broth. The addition of okra and gumbo file powder contributes to the gumbo's signature thickness and complexity. Serve it over rice for a satisfying and comforting Cajun-inspired meal!

Main Dishes - Meat:

Cajun Boudin Sausage

Ingredients:

For the Boudin Filling:

- 1 pound pork shoulder, cut into chunks
- 1/2 pound pork liver
- 1 large onion, chopped
- 1 bell pepper, chopped
- 2 celery stalks, chopped
- 3 cloves garlic, minced
- 1 cup cooked white rice
- 1/4 cup fresh parsley, chopped
- 1/4 cup green onions, chopped
- 1 teaspoon thyme
- 1 teaspoon cayenne pepper (adjust to taste)
- Salt and black pepper to taste
- 10 feet hog casings, soaked in water (for stuffing)

For the Boudin Sausage:

- Vegetable oil for cooking
- All-purpose flour (for dusting)
- Cooked white rice (for serving)
- Chopped green onions (for garnish)

Instructions:

1. Prepare the Boudin Filling:

- In a large pot, combine pork shoulder, pork liver, chopped onion, bell pepper, celery, and minced garlic. Cover with water and simmer until the meats are cooked through.

2. Grind Meat Mixture:

- Pass the cooked meat mixture through a meat grinder or food processor.

3. Mix with Rice and Herbs:

- In a large mixing bowl, combine the ground meat mixture with cooked white rice, fresh parsley, green onions, thyme, cayenne pepper, salt, and black pepper. Mix well.

4. Prepare Casings:

- Rinse hog casings thoroughly in running water. Soak them in water for about 30 minutes.

5. Stuff the Casings:

- Using a sausage stuffer or a funnel, stuff the hog casings with the boudin mixture. Twist into 6-inch links and tie the ends.

6. Cook the Boudin Sausages:

- Bring a pot of water to a gentle simmer. Place the boudin sausages in the simmering water and poach for about 30 minutes. This helps set the casings.

7. Sauté or Grill:

- Heat vegetable oil in a skillet or grill. Lightly dust the boudin sausages with flour and cook until browned on all sides.

8. Serve:

- Serve the Cajun Boudin Sausages over a bed of cooked white rice.
- Garnish with chopped green onions.

9. Enjoy:

- Enjoy these Cajun Boudin Sausages, a flavorful and spicy sausage with a unique blend of meats, rice, and aromatic herbs.

Cajun Boudin Sausage is a classic Louisiana delicacy, combining the richness of pork, the earthiness of liver, and the aromatic flavors of Cajun seasonings. The addition of rice gives it a distinctive texture and makes it a complete and satisfying dish. Whether sautéed or grilled, these boudin sausages offer a taste of authentic Cajun cuisine!

Pork Grillades and Grits

Ingredients:

For the Pork Grillades:

- 1 1/2 pounds pork shoulder or pork round steaks, thinly sliced
- 1/2 cup all-purpose flour
- Salt and black pepper to taste
- 1/4 cup vegetable oil
- 1 large onion, chopped
- 1 bell pepper, chopped
- 2 celery stalks, chopped
- 3 cloves garlic, minced
- 1 can (14 ounces) diced tomatoes, undrained
- 1 cup beef or chicken broth
- 1 teaspoon Worcestershire sauce
- 1 teaspoon hot sauce (adjust to taste)
- 1 teaspoon dried thyme
- 1 teaspoon dried oregano
- 1 bay leaf
- Chopped green onions (for garnish)
- Chopped fresh parsley (for garnish)

For the Grits:

- 1 cup stone-ground grits
- 4 cups water
- 1 teaspoon salt
- 1/2 cup heavy cream
- 4 tablespoons unsalted butter
- 1 cup shredded cheddar cheese

Instructions:

1. Prepare the Pork Grillades:

- Season the thinly sliced pork with salt and black pepper. Dredge the pork in flour, shaking off excess.

2. Brown the Pork:

- In a large skillet, heat vegetable oil over medium-high heat. Brown the pork slices on both sides. Remove from the skillet and set aside.

3. Sauté Vegetables:

- In the same skillet, add chopped onion, bell pepper, celery, and minced garlic. Sauté until the vegetables are softened.

4. Create Sauce:

- Stir in diced tomatoes, beef or chicken broth, Worcestershire sauce, hot sauce, dried thyme, dried oregano, and bay leaf. Mix well.

5. Simmer Grillades:

- Return the browned pork slices to the skillet. Bring the mixture to a simmer. Cover and let it simmer for about 1 to 1.5 hours or until the pork is tender.

6. Prepare the Grits:

- In a separate pot, bring water to a boil. Stir in stone-ground grits and salt. Reduce heat to low and simmer, stirring occasionally, until the grits are thickened.

7. Finish Grits:

- Stir in heavy cream, unsalted butter, and shredded cheddar cheese into the grits. Continue to cook until the grits are creamy and smooth.

8. Serve:

- Spoon a generous portion of grits onto each plate. Top with the pork grillades and sauce.

9. Garnish:

- Garnish with chopped green onions and fresh parsley.

10. Enjoy:

- Enjoy this comforting and hearty dish of Pork Grillades and Grits, a classic Southern favorite that combines tender pork in a flavorful tomato-based sauce served over creamy cheddar grits.

Pork Grillades and Grits is a soulful and satisfying dish that highlights the rich flavors of pork simmered in a savory Creole-inspired tomato gravy. Paired with creamy and cheesy grits, it's a comforting meal that captures the essence of Southern cuisine. Serve it for breakfast, brunch, or dinner to experience the warmth and flavor of traditional Southern cooking.

Cajun Meat Pies

Ingredients:

For the Dough:

- 3 cups all-purpose flour
- 1 teaspoon salt
- 1 cup cold unsalted butter, cut into small cubes
- 1/2 cup ice-cold water

For the Filling:

- 1 pound ground beef or pork
- 1/2 pound Andouille sausage, finely chopped
- 1 large onion, finely chopped
- 1 bell pepper, finely chopped
- 2 celery stalks, finely chopped
- 3 cloves garlic, minced
- 1 can (14 ounces) diced tomatoes, drained
- 1 teaspoon Cajun seasoning
- 1/2 teaspoon dried thyme
- 1/2 teaspoon dried oregano
- 1/4 teaspoon cayenne pepper (adjust to taste)
- Salt and black pepper to taste
- Vegetable oil for frying

Instructions:

1. Prepare the Dough:

- In a large bowl, combine flour and salt. Add the cold, cubed butter and use a pastry cutter or your hands to mix until the mixture resembles coarse crumbs.
- Gradually add cold water, a little at a time, and mix until the dough comes together. Form it into a ball, wrap in plastic wrap, and refrigerate for at least 1 hour.

2. Make the Filling:

- In a skillet, cook ground beef or pork and Andouille sausage over medium heat until browned. Drain excess fat.
- Add chopped onion, bell pepper, celery, and minced garlic. Cook until the vegetables are softened.
- Stir in diced tomatoes, Cajun seasoning, dried thyme, dried oregano, cayenne pepper, salt, and black pepper. Cook for an additional 5 minutes. Remove from heat and let it cool.

3. Roll Out the Dough:

- Preheat the oil for frying in a deep fryer or large, deep skillet to 350°F (175°C).
- On a floured surface, roll out the chilled dough to about 1/8-inch thickness. Cut out circles using a round cutter (approximately 4-6 inches in diameter).

4. Fill and Seal:

- Place a spoonful of the meat filling onto one half of each dough circle. Fold the other half over the filling, creating a half-moon shape.
- Seal the edges by pressing with a fork or your fingers.

5. Fry the Cajun Meat Pies:

- Carefully lower the pies into the hot oil and fry until golden brown, about 3-5 minutes per side.

6. Drain and Serve:

- Remove the fried Cajun Meat Pies and place them on paper towels to drain excess oil.

7. Enjoy:

- Serve the Cajun Meat Pies hot and enjoy the flavorful and savory filling encased in a golden, crispy crust.

Cajun Meat Pies are a delightful and portable way to enjoy the bold flavors of Cajun cuisine. These handheld pies are filled with a savory mixture of meat and vegetables, encased in a flaky and golden crust. Whether served as a snack, appetizer, or part of a festive spread, these Cajun Meat Pies are sure to be a hit with their delicious taste and convenient form.

Creole Beef Daube

Ingredients:

- 2 pounds beef chuck roast, cut into 2-inch cubes
- Salt and black pepper to taste
- 1/2 cup all-purpose flour
- 3 tablespoons vegetable oil
- 1 large onion, chopped
- 2 bell peppers, chopped
- 3 celery stalks, chopped
- 4 cloves garlic, minced
- 1 cup red wine (preferably a dry red)
- 1 can (14 ounces) diced tomatoes, undrained
- 1 cup beef broth
- 2 tablespoons tomato paste
- 2 teaspoons Worcestershire sauce
- 1 teaspoon dried thyme
- 1 teaspoon dried oregano
- 1 bay leaf
- 1/2 teaspoon cayenne pepper (adjust to taste)
- 1/2 teaspoon paprika
- 1/4 cup chopped fresh parsley (for garnish)
- Cooked rice (for serving)

Instructions:

1. Season and Flour Beef:

- Season beef cubes with salt and black pepper. Dredge the beef in flour, shaking off excess.

2. Brown Beef:

- In a large, heavy pot or Dutch oven, heat vegetable oil over medium-high heat. Brown the beef cubes on all sides. Work in batches to avoid overcrowding the pot. Remove browned beef and set aside.

3. Sauté Vegetables:

- In the same pot, add chopped onion, bell peppers, celery, and minced garlic. Sauté until the vegetables are softened.

4. Deglaze Pot:

- Pour red wine into the pot, scraping the bottom to release any browned bits. Allow the wine to simmer for a few minutes.

5. Add Tomatoes and Broth:

- Stir in diced tomatoes with their juice, beef broth, and tomato paste.

6. Season and Simmer:

- Add Worcestershire sauce, dried thyme, dried oregano, bay leaf, cayenne pepper, and paprika. Mix well. Return the browned beef to the pot.

7. Slow Cook:

- Bring the mixture to a simmer, then reduce the heat to low. Cover and let it simmer for about 2 to 2.5 hours or until the beef is tender.

8. Adjust Seasoning:

- Taste and adjust the seasoning with salt, black pepper, and additional cayenne pepper if desired.

9. Garnish and Serve:

- Remove the bay leaf. Garnish the Creole Beef Daube with chopped fresh parsley.

10. Serve:

- Serve the Creole Beef Daube over a bed of cooked rice.

11. Enjoy:

- Enjoy this rich and flavorful Creole Beef Daube, a comforting dish with tender beef, aromatic spices, and a savory tomato-based sauce.

Creole Beef Daube is a classic Louisiana dish that combines slow-cooked beef with a flavorful blend of Creole seasonings and vegetables. The result is a hearty and satisfying dish that pairs wonderfully with rice. This Creole-inspired beef stew captures the essence of Southern comfort food and is perfect for a cozy family dinner or special occasions.

Andouille and Chicken Jambalaya

Ingredients:

- 1 pound Andouille sausage, sliced
- 1 pound boneless, skinless chicken thighs, cut into bite-sized pieces
- Salt and black pepper to taste
- 2 tablespoons vegetable oil
- 1 large onion, finely chopped
- 1 bell pepper, finely chopped
- 2 celery stalks, finely chopped
- 3 cloves garlic, minced
- 1 can (14 ounces) diced tomatoes, undrained
- 1 cup long-grain white rice
- 2 cups chicken broth
- 1 teaspoon dried thyme
- 1 teaspoon dried oregano
- 1 teaspoon paprika
- 1/2 teaspoon cayenne pepper (adjust to taste)
- 2 bay leaves
- Chopped green onions (for garnish)
- Chopped fresh parsley (for garnish)

Instructions:

1. Season Meat:

   - Season the chicken pieces with salt and black pepper.

2. Brown Sausage and Chicken:

   - In a large pot or Dutch oven, heat vegetable oil over medium-high heat. Brown the Andouille sausage slices and chicken pieces. Remove and set aside.

3. Sauté Vegetables:

- In the same pot, add chopped onion, bell pepper, celery, and minced garlic. Sauté until the vegetables are softened.

4. Add Tomatoes and Rice:

- Stir in diced tomatoes with their juice. Add long-grain white rice and mix well.

5. Combine Meat and Broth:

- Return the browned Andouille sausage and chicken to the pot. Pour in chicken broth.

6. Season and Simmer:

- Add dried thyme, dried oregano, paprika, cayenne pepper, and bay leaves. Mix thoroughly. Bring the mixture to a boil, then reduce the heat to low. Cover and let it simmer for about 20-25 minutes or until the rice is cooked and the liquid is absorbed.

7. Adjust Seasoning:

- Taste and adjust the seasoning with salt, black pepper, and cayenne pepper if needed.

8. Garnish and Serve:

- Remove the bay leaves. Garnish the Andouille and Chicken Jambalaya with chopped green onions and fresh parsley.

9. Serve:

- Serve the Jambalaya hot, either in bowls or plated, and enjoy the flavorful blend of Andouille sausage, chicken, and aromatic spices.

10. Enjoy:

- Enjoy this Andouille and Chicken Jambalaya, a classic Louisiana dish that brings together the vibrant flavors of Creole cuisine in a hearty and satisfying one-pot meal.

This Andouille and Chicken Jambalaya is a quintessential dish from the heart of Cajun and Creole cooking. With a medley of spices, chicken, and the distinctive flavor of Andouille sausage, this jambalaya captures the essence of Louisiana cuisine. It's a comforting and flavorful dish that is perfect for sharing with family and friends.

Dirty Rice with Ground Beef and Pork

Ingredients:

- 1 cup long-grain white rice
- 1 1/2 cups chicken broth
- 1/2 pound ground beef
- 1/2 pound ground pork
- Salt and black pepper to taste
- 2 tablespoons vegetable oil
- 1 large onion, finely chopped
- 1 bell pepper, finely chopped
- 2 celery stalks, finely chopped
- 3 cloves garlic, minced
- 2 green onions, chopped (for garnish)
- Chopped fresh parsley (for garnish)

For the Cajun Seasoning:

- 1 teaspoon paprika
- 1 teaspoon onion powder
- 1 teaspoon garlic powder
- 1 teaspoon dried thyme
- 1 teaspoon dried oregano
- 1/2 teaspoon cayenne pepper (adjust to taste)
- Salt and black pepper to taste

Instructions:

1. Cook Rice:

- In a saucepan, combine the rice and chicken broth. Bring to a boil, then reduce heat to low, cover, and simmer until the rice is cooked and the liquid is absorbed.

2. Prepare Cajun Seasoning:

- In a small bowl, mix together paprika, onion powder, garlic powder, dried thyme, dried oregano, cayenne pepper, salt, and black pepper. Set aside.

3. Brown Meat:

- In a large skillet, brown the ground beef and ground pork over medium-high heat. Season with salt, black pepper, and half of the Cajun seasoning. Cook until the meat is browned and cooked through. Drain excess fat.

4. Sauté Vegetables:

- In the same skillet, heat vegetable oil over medium heat. Add chopped onion, bell pepper, celery, and minced garlic. Sauté until the vegetables are softened.

5. Combine Rice and Meat:

- Add the cooked rice to the skillet with the sautéed vegetables. Mix well.

6. Season and Mix:

- Sprinkle the remaining Cajun seasoning over the rice and meat mixture. Stir until everything is well combined.

7. Adjust Seasoning:

- Taste and adjust the seasoning with additional salt, black pepper, or Cajun seasoning if needed.

8. Garnish and Serve:

- Garnish the Dirty Rice with chopped green onions and fresh parsley.

9. Enjoy:

- Serve the Dirty Rice with Ground Beef and Pork hot as a flavorful side dish or a satisfying main course.

Tip: For an extra kick, you can add hot sauce or additional cayenne pepper according to your spice preference.

This Dirty Rice recipe with a combination of ground beef and pork brings a bold and savory Cajun flavor to the table. The mix of aromatic spices, vegetables, and perfectly cooked rice creates a delicious and satisfying dish. Whether served as a side or a main course, this Dirty Rice is sure to be a hit with its rich and comforting flavors.

Side Dishes:

Cajun Corn Maque Choux

Ingredients:

- 4 cups fresh or frozen corn kernels
- 1/2 pound Andouille sausage, diced
- 1 large onion, finely chopped
- 1 bell pepper, finely chopped
- 2 celery stalks, finely chopped
- 3 cloves garlic, minced
- 1 cup cherry tomatoes, halved
- 1/2 cup green onions, chopped
- 1/4 cup fresh parsley, chopped
- 1 cup heavy cream
- 2 tablespoons vegetable oil
- Salt and black pepper to taste
- Cajun seasoning to taste
- Hot sauce (optional, for added spice)

Instructions:

1. Sauté Vegetables and Sausage:

    - In a large skillet, heat vegetable oil over medium heat. Add diced Andouille sausage and sauté until browned.

2. Add Aromatics:

    - Add chopped onion, bell pepper, and celery to the skillet. Sauté until the vegetables are softened.

3. Incorporate Garlic:

    - Stir in minced garlic and cook for an additional minute until fragrant.

4. Cook Corn:

- Add corn kernels to the skillet and cook for about 5-7 minutes, allowing them to caramelize slightly.

5. Add Tomatoes and Seasoning:

    - Toss in cherry tomatoes and season the mixture with salt, black pepper, Cajun seasoning, and hot sauce (if using). Adjust the spice level according to your preference.

6. Pour in Heavy Cream:

    - Pour heavy cream over the corn mixture and stir well to combine.

7. Simmer:

    - Reduce heat to low and let the mixture simmer for about 10-15 minutes, allowing the flavors to meld and the cream to thicken.

8. Finish with Herbs:

    - Stir in chopped green onions and fresh parsley. Cook for an additional 2-3 minutes.

9. Adjust Seasoning:

    - Taste the Cajun Corn Maque Choux and adjust the seasoning if needed. Add more salt, black pepper, or Cajun seasoning according to your taste.

10. Serve:

    - Serve the Cajun Corn Maque Choux hot as a side dish or over rice.

11. Enjoy:

    - Enjoy the rich and flavorful Cajun Corn Maque Choux, a delightful combination of sweet corn, savory Andouille sausage, and aromatic spices.

Cajun Corn Maque Choux is a classic Louisiana dish that showcases the vibrant flavors of Cajun cuisine. This side dish, featuring sweet corn, Andouille sausage, and a creamy base, is a perfect accompaniment to a variety of main courses. Whether served at a family dinner or a festive gathering, this dish is sure to add a touch of Southern comfort to your table.

Creole Mustard Potato Salad

Ingredients:

- 2 pounds red potatoes, washed and cut into bite-sized cubes
- 1/2 cup mayonnaise
- 3 tablespoons Creole mustard
- 1 tablespoon Dijon mustard
- 2 tablespoons apple cider vinegar
- 1 tablespoon sugar
- 1 teaspoon Cajun seasoning
- Salt and black pepper to taste
- 1/2 cup celery, finely chopped
- 1/4 cup red onion, finely chopped
- 1/4 cup green bell pepper, finely chopped
- 2 hard-boiled eggs, chopped (optional, for garnish)
- Paprika (for garnish)

Instructions:

1. Boil Potatoes:

- Place the potato cubes in a pot of salted water. Bring to a boil and cook until the potatoes are fork-tender but still firm. Drain and let them cool.

2. Prepare Dressing:

- In a bowl, whisk together mayonnaise, Creole mustard, Dijon mustard, apple cider vinegar, sugar, Cajun seasoning, salt, and black pepper. Adjust the seasonings to your taste.

3. Combine Potatoes and Dressing:

- Place the cooled potato cubes in a large mixing bowl. Pour the dressing over the potatoes and gently toss until the potatoes are evenly coated.

4. Add Vegetables:

- Add finely chopped celery, red onion, and green bell pepper to the bowl. Mix well to combine.

5. Chill:

- Cover the bowl with plastic wrap and refrigerate the Creole Mustard Potato Salad for at least 2 hours to allow the flavors to meld.

6. Garnish:

- If desired, garnish the potato salad with chopped hard-boiled eggs and a sprinkle of paprika before serving.

7. Serve:

- Serve the Creole Mustard Potato Salad chilled as a flavorful side dish.

8. Enjoy:

- Enjoy this zesty and tangy Creole Mustard Potato Salad, perfect for picnics, barbecues, or as a side for any meal.

Creole Mustard Potato Salad offers a bold and flavorful twist on the classic potato salad. The combination of Creole and Dijon mustards, along with Cajun seasoning, adds a zesty and spicy kick to the creamy dressing. With the addition of crunchy vegetables, this potato salad is a delightful side dish that complements a variety of main courses. It's a taste of the vibrant flavors of Creole cuisine in a classic picnic favorite.

Red Beans and Rice

Ingredients:

- 1 pound dried red kidney beans
- 1 tablespoon vegetable oil
- 1 large onion, finely chopped
- 1 bell pepper, finely chopped
- 2 celery stalks, finely chopped
- 3 cloves garlic, minced
- 1 pound Andouille sausage, sliced
- 1 ham hock or smoked ham shank
- 1 teaspoon dried thyme
- 2 bay leaves
- 1 teaspoon Cajun seasoning
- 1/2 teaspoon cayenne pepper (adjust to taste)
- Salt and black pepper to taste
- 6 cups chicken broth
- 4 cups cooked white rice
- Chopped green onions (for garnish)
- Chopped fresh parsley (for garnish)

Instructions:

1. Prepare the Beans:

- Rinse the dried red kidney beans and soak them overnight in water. Alternatively, use the quick soak method by bringing the beans to a boil, then letting them sit for 1 hour before draining.

2. Sauté Vegetables:

- In a large pot or Dutch oven, heat vegetable oil over medium heat. Add chopped onion, bell pepper, celery, and minced garlic. Sauté until the vegetables are softened.

3. Brown Sausage:

- Add sliced Andouille sausage to the pot and cook until browned.

4. Add Beans and Ham:

    - Stir in soaked and drained red kidney beans. Add the ham hock or smoked ham shank.

5. Season:

    - Season with dried thyme, bay leaves, Cajun seasoning, cayenne pepper, salt, and black pepper. Mix well.

6. Pour Broth:

    - Pour in chicken broth and bring the mixture to a boil.

7. Simmer:

    - Reduce heat to low, cover the pot, and let it simmer for 2 to 2.5 hours or until the beans are tender, stirring occasionally.

8. Mash Beans (Optional):

    - If desired, mash some of the beans against the side of the pot to thicken the mixture.

9. Adjust Seasoning:

    - Taste and adjust the seasoning with salt, black pepper, and cayenne pepper if needed.

10. Serve:

    - Serve the Red Beans and Rice over a bed of cooked white rice.

11. Garnish:

    - Garnish with chopped green onions and fresh parsley.

12. Enjoy:

- Enjoy this classic and comforting dish of Red Beans and Rice, a staple in Creole and Cajun cuisine.

Red Beans and Rice is a traditional and hearty dish that holds a special place in the heart of Louisiana cuisine. The combination of red kidney beans, Andouille sausage, and aromatic seasonings creates a flavorful and satisfying meal. Served over a bed of white rice, this dish is a celebration of rich flavors and cultural heritage. Whether enjoyed for a weeknight dinner or as part of a festive gathering, Red Beans and Rice is a true taste of Louisiana comfort.

Collard Greens with Andouille

Ingredients:

- 2 bunches collard greens, washed, stems removed, and chopped
- 1 pound Andouille sausage, sliced
- 2 tablespoons vegetable oil
- 1 large onion, finely chopped
- 3 cloves garlic, minced
- 1 teaspoon smoked paprika
- 1 teaspoon Cajun seasoning
- 1/2 teaspoon red pepper flakes (adjust to taste)
- Salt and black pepper to taste
- 3 cups chicken broth
- 1 cup water
- 1 tablespoon apple cider vinegar
- Hot sauce (optional, for serving)

Instructions:

1. Prepare Collard Greens:

- Wash the collard greens thoroughly, remove the tough stems, and chop the leaves.

2. Sauté Andouille:

- In a large pot or Dutch oven, heat vegetable oil over medium heat. Add sliced Andouille sausage and cook until browned.

3. Add Aromatics:

- Add finely chopped onion and minced garlic to the pot. Sauté until the onions are translucent.

4. Season:

- Sprinkle smoked paprika, Cajun seasoning, red pepper flakes, salt, and black pepper over the sausage and vegetables. Mix well to coat.

5. Incorporate Collard Greens:

   - Add the chopped collard greens to the pot and stir until they start to wilt.

6. Pour Liquids:

   - Pour in chicken broth, water, and apple cider vinegar. Stir to combine.

7. Simmer:

   - Bring the mixture to a simmer. Reduce heat to low, cover, and let it simmer for about 45 minutes to 1 hour, stirring occasionally.

8. Check and Adjust:

   - Check the collard greens for tenderness. If needed, continue simmering until they reach your desired level of tenderness.

9. Serve:

   - Serve the Collard Greens with Andouille hot as a flavorful side dish.

10. Optional:

    - Drizzle with hot sauce before serving for an extra kick.

11. Enjoy:

    - Enjoy this Southern classic of Collard Greens with Andouille, a dish that combines the smoky and spicy flavors of Andouille sausage with the hearty and nutritious collard greens.

Collard Greens with Andouille is a staple in Southern cuisine, combining the earthy richness of collard greens with the smoky and spicy kick of Andouille sausage. This dish is not only delicious but also a nutritious and satisfying addition to any meal. Serve it alongside cornbread or as a side to your favorite Southern-inspired main course for a true taste of the South.

Cajun Dirty Rice

Ingredients:

- 1 cup long-grain white rice
- 2 cups chicken broth
- 1/2 pound chicken livers, finely chopped
- 1/2 pound ground pork
- 1/2 pound Andouille sausage, finely chopped
- 1 onion, finely chopped
- 1 bell pepper, finely chopped
- 2 celery stalks, finely chopped
- 3 cloves garlic, minced
- 3 green onions, chopped
- 1/4 cup fresh parsley, chopped
- 1 teaspoon Cajun seasoning
- 1/2 teaspoon dried thyme
- 1/2 teaspoon paprika
- 1/4 teaspoon cayenne pepper (adjust to taste)
- Salt and black pepper to taste
- 2 tablespoons vegetable oil

Instructions:

1. Cook Rice:

- In a saucepan, combine the rice and chicken broth. Bring to a boil, then reduce heat to low, cover, and simmer until the rice is cooked and the liquid is absorbed.

2. Sauté Meats:

- In a large skillet, heat vegetable oil over medium-high heat. Add chopped chicken livers, ground pork, and chopped Andouille sausage. Cook until browned.

3. Add Vegetables:

- Stir in chopped onion, bell pepper, celery, and minced garlic. Sauté until the vegetables are softened.

4. Season:

- Season the mixture with Cajun seasoning, dried thyme, paprika, cayenne pepper, salt, and black pepper. Mix well.

5. Combine Rice and Meats:

- Add the cooked rice to the skillet with the sautéed meats and vegetables. Mix thoroughly.

6. Finish with Herbs:

- Stir in chopped green onions and fresh parsley. Cook for an additional 2-3 minutes.

7. Adjust Seasoning:

- Taste the Cajun Dirty Rice and adjust the seasoning if needed. Add more salt, black pepper, or cayenne pepper according to your taste.

8. Serve:

- Serve the Cajun Dirty Rice hot as a flavorful side dish.

9. Enjoy:

- Enjoy this savory and spiced Cajun Dirty Rice, a classic Louisiana dish that brings together a medley of meats, vegetables, and aromatic seasonings.

Cajun Dirty Rice is a beloved dish in Cajun and Creole cuisine, known for its flavorful combination of meats, vegetables, and spices. The name "dirty rice" comes from the color of the dish, created by the mix of ingredients. Whether served as a side dish or a main course, this Cajun Dirty Rice is sure to satisfy your taste buds with its rich and savory profile.

Baked Macaroni and Cheese

Ingredients:

- 8 ounces elbow macaroni or your favorite pasta
- 1/4 cup unsalted butter
- 1/4 cup all-purpose flour
- 1/2 teaspoon salt
- 1/4 teaspoon black pepper
- 1/4 teaspoon onion powder
- 1/4 teaspoon mustard powder
- 1/4 teaspoon cayenne pepper (optional, for a kick)
- 2 1/2 cups milk
- 2 cups shredded sharp cheddar cheese
- 1/2 cup shredded mozzarella cheese
- 1/2 cup grated Parmesan cheese
- 1/2 cup breadcrumbs (optional, for topping)
- Chopped fresh parsley (for garnish)

Instructions:

1. Cook Pasta:

- Cook the elbow macaroni or your preferred pasta according to the package instructions. Drain and set aside.

2. Preheat Oven:

- Preheat your oven to 350°F (175°C).

3. Make Cheese Sauce:

- In a medium saucepan, melt the butter over medium heat. Stir in the flour, salt, black pepper, onion powder, mustard powder, and cayenne pepper (if using) to create a roux.
- Gradually whisk in the milk until the mixture is smooth and begins to thicken.

4. Add Cheese:

   - Reduce the heat to low, then add the shredded cheddar, mozzarella, and grated Parmesan cheese. Stir until the cheese is melted and the sauce is creamy.

5. Combine Pasta and Cheese Sauce:

   - In a large mixing bowl, combine the cooked pasta with the cheese sauce. Mix until the pasta is evenly coated.

6. Transfer to Baking Dish:

   - Transfer the macaroni and cheese mixture to a greased baking dish, spreading it out evenly.

7. Optional Topping:

   - If desired, sprinkle breadcrumbs evenly over the top of the macaroni and cheese for a crunchy topping.

8. Bake:

   - Bake in the preheated oven for about 25-30 minutes or until the top is golden brown and the edges are bubbly.

9. Garnish and Serve:

   - Remove from the oven and let it rest for a few minutes. Garnish with chopped fresh parsley.

10. Enjoy:

    - Serve the Baked Macaroni and Cheese hot as a comforting and cheesy dish that's perfect for any occasion.

Baked Macaroni and Cheese is a classic comfort food that never goes out of style. This recipe delivers a rich and creamy cheese sauce paired with perfectly cooked pasta, baked to golden perfection. Whether served as a side dish or the main attraction, this Baked Macaroni and Cheese is sure to be a hit at family gatherings, potlucks, or any time you're craving a hearty and delicious meal.

Vegetarian/Vegan:

Vegan Gumbo

Ingredients:

For the Roux:

- 1/2 cup vegetable oil
- 1/2 cup all-purpose flour

Vegetables and Aromatics:

- 1 large onion, diced
- 1 bell pepper, diced
- 2 celery stalks, diced
- 3 cloves garlic, minced

Vegetables and Proteins:

- 1 cup okra, sliced
- 1 cup tomatoes, diced
- 1 cup eggplant, diced
- 1 cup carrots, diced
- 1 cup zucchini, diced
- 1 cup corn kernels
- 1 can (15 ounces) kidney beans, drained and rinsed
- 1 can (15 ounces) chickpeas, drained and rinsed
- 1 cup chopped collard greens or kale

Spices and Seasonings:

- 1 teaspoon dried thyme
- 1 teaspoon dried oregano
- 1 teaspoon smoked paprika
- 1/2 teaspoon cayenne pepper (adjust to taste)
- Salt and black pepper to taste
- 1 bay leaf

Liquid Ingredients:

- 8 cups vegetable broth
- 1 can (14 ounces) diced tomatoes, undrained

For Serving:

- Cooked white rice
- Chopped green onions (for garnish)
- Chopped fresh parsley (for garnish)
- Hot sauce (optional)

Instructions:

1. Prepare the Roux:

- In a large pot, heat vegetable oil over medium heat. Gradually whisk in the flour to create a roux. Stir continuously until the roux becomes a dark, chocolate-brown color. Be attentive to prevent burning.

2. Sauté Vegetables and Aromatics:

- Add diced onion, bell pepper, celery, and minced garlic to the pot with the roux. Sauté until the vegetables are softened.

3. Add Vegetables and Proteins:

- Stir in sliced okra, diced tomatoes, diced eggplant, diced carrots, diced zucchini, corn kernels, kidney beans, chickpeas, and chopped collard greens (or kale).

4. Season:

- Add dried thyme, dried oregano, smoked paprika, cayenne pepper, salt, black pepper, and bay leaf. Mix well to coat the vegetables.

5. Pour in Liquids:

- Pour in vegetable broth and diced tomatoes (with their juice). Stir to combine.

6. Simmer:

- Bring the mixture to a boil, then reduce heat to low. Cover and let it simmer for about 30-40 minutes to allow the flavors to meld.

7. Adjust Seasoning:

- Taste the Vegan Gumbo and adjust the seasoning if needed. Add more salt, black pepper, or cayenne pepper according to your taste.

8. Serve:

- Serve the Vegan Gumbo over a bed of cooked white rice.

9. Garnish:

- Garnish with chopped green onions and fresh parsley. Add hot sauce if desired.

10. Enjoy:

- Enjoy this hearty and flavorful Vegan Gumbo, a plant-based twist on the classic Louisiana dish.

Vegan Gumbo is a delicious and satisfying plant-based version of the traditional Louisiana stew. Packed with a variety of vegetables, beans, and flavorful spices, this vegan rendition captures the essence of Gumbo without the need for animal products. Serve it over a bed of rice for a wholesome and comforting meal that celebrates the rich flavors of Cajun and Creole cuisine.

Cajun-Style Stuffed Bell Peppers

Ingredients:

- 4 large bell peppers, halved and seeds removed
- 1 cup long-grain white rice, cooked
- 1 pound ground beef or plant-based alternative (e.g., Beyond Meat)
- 1 onion, finely chopped
- 2 celery stalks, finely chopped
- 3 cloves garlic, minced
- 1 can (14 ounces) diced tomatoes, drained
- 1 cup corn kernels (fresh or frozen)
- 1 cup black beans, drained and rinsed
- 1 teaspoon Cajun seasoning
- 1/2 teaspoon dried thyme
- 1/2 teaspoon smoked paprika
- Salt and black pepper to taste
- 1 cup shredded cheddar or vegan cheese
- Chopped green onions (for garnish)
- Chopped fresh parsley (for garnish)

Instructions:

1. Preheat the Oven:

- Preheat your oven to 375°F (190°C).

2. Prepare Bell Peppers:

- Cut the bell peppers in half lengthwise, removing seeds and membranes. Place them in a baking dish.

3. Cook Rice:

- Cook the long-grain white rice according to package instructions. Set aside.

4. Sauté Vegetables:

- In a large skillet, cook the ground beef (or plant-based alternative) over medium heat until browned. Add chopped onion, celery, and minced garlic. Sauté until the vegetables are softened.

5. Add Tomatoes, Corn, and Beans:

- Stir in diced tomatoes, corn kernels, and black beans. Cook for a few minutes until the mixture is well combined.

6. Season:

- Add Cajun seasoning, dried thyme, smoked paprika, salt, and black pepper. Mix well.

7. Combine Rice:

- Fold in the cooked rice, making sure all ingredients are evenly distributed.

8. Stuff Bell Peppers:

- Spoon the filling mixture into the halved bell peppers, pressing down to pack the filling.

9. Top with Cheese:

- Sprinkle shredded cheddar or vegan cheese over the top of each stuffed bell pepper.

10. Bake:

- Cover the baking dish with foil and bake in the preheated oven for 25-30 minutes, or until the bell peppers are tender.

11. Garnish:

- Remove from the oven and garnish with chopped green onions and fresh parsley.

12. Serve:

- Serve the Cajun-Style Stuffed Bell Peppers hot as a flavorful and satisfying dish.

13. Enjoy:

- Enjoy this Cajun-inspired twist on classic stuffed peppers, bringing a spicy kick and a mix of bold flavors to your table.

Cajun-Style Stuffed Bell Peppers offer a flavorful and hearty dish with a touch of Louisiana-inspired spice. The combination of seasoned ground beef or plant-based alternative, rice, and a variety of vegetables, all topped with melted cheese, creates a delicious and satisfying meal. Whether served as a main course or a side dish, these stuffed peppers are sure to add a taste of Cajun cuisine to your dining experience.

Creole eggplant Casserole

Ingredients:

- 2 large eggplants, peeled and diced
- 1 tablespoon salt
- 2 tablespoons olive oil
- 1 onion, finely chopped
- 1 bell pepper, finely chopped
- 2 celery stalks, finely chopped
- 3 cloves garlic, minced
- 1 can (14 ounces) diced tomatoes, drained
- 1 cup tomato sauce
- 1 teaspoon dried thyme
- 1 teaspoon dried oregano
- 1 teaspoon smoked paprika
- 1/2 teaspoon cayenne pepper (adjust to taste)
- Salt and black pepper to taste
- 1 cup cooked andouille sausage or plant-based sausage, diced (optional)
- 1 cup breadcrumbs
- 1/2 cup chopped fresh parsley
- 1 cup shredded cheddar or vegan cheese

Instructions:

1. Preheat the Oven:

- Preheat your oven to 375°F (190°C).

2. Prepare Eggplants:

- Place diced eggplants in a colander, sprinkle with salt, and let them drain for about 30 minutes. This helps remove excess moisture.

3. Sauté Vegetables:

- In a large skillet, heat olive oil over medium heat. Add chopped onion, bell pepper, celery, and minced garlic. Sauté until the vegetables are softened.

4. Add Tomatoes and Seasoning:

    - Stir in diced tomatoes, tomato sauce, dried thyme, dried oregano, smoked paprika, cayenne pepper, salt, and black pepper. Cook for a few minutes to allow the flavors to meld.

5. Cook Eggplants:

    - Pat the drained eggplants dry and add them to the skillet. Cook until the eggplants are tender.

6. Add Sausage (Optional):

    - If using andouille sausage or plant-based sausage, add the diced sausage to the skillet. Cook until heated through.

7. Assemble Casserole:

    - Transfer the mixture to a greased baking dish. Sprinkle half of the breadcrumbs and half of the chopped parsley over the mixture.

8. Top with Cheese:

    - Sprinkle shredded cheddar or vegan cheese over the breadcrumbs.

9. Finish Assembling:

    - Top with the remaining breadcrumbs and chopped parsley.

10. Bake:

    - Bake in the preheated oven for 25-30 minutes or until the top is golden brown and the casserole is bubbly.

11. Serve:

    - Remove from the oven and let it rest for a few minutes before serving.

12. Enjoy:

    - Serve the Creole Eggplant Casserole hot as a flavorful and comforting dish.

Creole Eggplant Casserole is a delightful combination of diced eggplants, a medley of vegetables, and a flavorful Creole-inspired tomato sauce. Whether you include andouille sausage or opt for a plant-based version, this casserole is a delicious and comforting way to enjoy the rich flavors of Creole cuisine. Topped with breadcrumbs and melted cheese, it's a hearty dish that can be served as a main course or a flavorful side dish.

Red Beans and Rice (Vegetarian Version)

Ingredients:

- 1 cup dried red kidney beans
- 2 tablespoons olive oil
- 1 large onion, finely chopped
- 1 bell pepper, finely chopped
- 2 celery stalks, finely chopped
- 3 cloves garlic, minced
- 1 teaspoon dried thyme
- 2 bay leaves
- 1 teaspoon smoked paprika
- 1/2 teaspoon cayenne pepper (adjust to taste)
- Salt and black pepper to taste
- 4 cups vegetable broth
- 1 can (14 ounces) diced tomatoes, undrained
- 2 cups cooked white rice
- Chopped green onions (for garnish)
- Chopped fresh parsley (for garnish)

Instructions:

1. Prepare the Beans:

- Rinse the dried red kidney beans and soak them overnight in water. Alternatively, use the quick soak method by bringing the beans to a boil, then letting them sit for 1 hour before draining.

2. Sauté Vegetables:

- In a large pot or Dutch oven, heat olive oil over medium heat. Add chopped onion, bell pepper, celery, and minced garlic. Sauté until the vegetables are softened.

3. Add Spices:

- Stir in dried thyme, bay leaves, smoked paprika, cayenne pepper, salt, and black pepper. Mix well to coat the vegetables with the spices.

4. Cook Beans:

- Add the soaked and drained red kidney beans to the pot. Pour in vegetable broth and diced tomatoes with their juice. Bring the mixture to a boil.

5. Simmer:

- Reduce heat to low, cover the pot, and let it simmer for 1.5 to 2 hours or until the beans are tender. Stir occasionally.

6. Mash Beans (Optional):

- If desired, mash some of the beans against the side of the pot to thicken the mixture.

7. Adjust Seasoning:

- Taste the Vegetarian Red Beans and Rice and adjust the seasoning with salt, black pepper, or cayenne pepper if needed.

8. Serve:

- Serve the red beans over a bed of cooked white rice.

9. Garnish:

- Garnish with chopped green onions and fresh parsley.

10. Enjoy:

- Enjoy this flavorful Vegetarian Red Beans and Rice as a wholesome and satisfying meal.

Vegetarian Red Beans and Rice offer a meat-free version of the classic Louisiana dish while retaining the rich and savory flavors. This hearty and satisfying meal combines red kidney beans with a medley of vegetables and aromatic spices. Served over a bed of white rice, it's a comforting and nutritious dish that captures the essence of traditional Creole cuisine. Garnish with green onions and fresh parsley for a delightful finishing touch.

Okra and Tomatoes

Ingredients:

- 1 pound fresh okra, washed and sliced
- 2 tablespoons vegetable oil
- 1 onion, finely chopped
- 2 cloves garlic, minced
- 4 large tomatoes, diced
- 1 bell pepper, diced
- 1 teaspoon dried thyme
- 1 teaspoon smoked paprika
- 1/2 teaspoon cayenne pepper (adjust to taste)
- Salt and black pepper to taste
- Chopped fresh parsley (for garnish)

Instructions:

1. Prepare Okra:

   - Wash the okra and trim the ends. Slice the okra into 1/2-inch pieces.

2. Sauté Okra:

   - In a large skillet, heat vegetable oil over medium heat. Add sliced okra and sauté for about 5-7 minutes or until it starts to brown. Stir occasionally to prevent sticking.

3. Add Aromatics:

   - Add chopped onion and minced garlic to the skillet. Sauté until the onions are translucent.

4. Incorporate Tomatoes and Bell Pepper:

   - Stir in diced tomatoes and bell pepper. Cook for an additional 5-7 minutes until the tomatoes release their juices.

5. Season:

- Season the mixture with dried thyme, smoked paprika, cayenne pepper, salt, and black pepper. Adjust the seasoning to your taste.

6. Simmer:

    - Reduce the heat to low, cover the skillet, and let the mixture simmer for about 15-20 minutes, allowing the flavors to meld.

7. Check Okra Tenderness:

    - Check the tenderness of the okra. Continue simmering if needed until the okra reaches your desired level of tenderness.

8. Garnish:

    - Garnish the Okra and Tomatoes with chopped fresh parsley.

9. Serve:

    - Serve as a flavorful side dish or over rice as a main course.

10. Enjoy:

    - Enjoy this simple and delicious Okra and Tomatoes dish that highlights the natural flavors of fresh okra and ripe tomatoes.

Okra and Tomatoes is a classic Southern dish that celebrates the combination of tender okra and juicy tomatoes. This simple and flavorful recipe brings out the best in these two ingredients with the addition of aromatic spices. Whether served as a side dish or a vegetarian main course, Okra and Tomatoes is a delicious and comforting way to enjoy the bounty of the garden. Garnish with fresh parsley for a burst of color and freshness.

Breads:

New Orleans-Style French Bread

Ingredients:

- 1 1/2 cups warm water (110°F/43°C)
- 1 tablespoon sugar
- 2 1/4 teaspoons active dry yeast (1 packet)
- 4 cups bread flour
- 1 1/2 teaspoons salt
- Cornmeal (for dusting)

Instructions:

1. Activate the Yeast:

   - In a small bowl, combine warm water and sugar. Stir until the sugar dissolves. Sprinkle the yeast over the water and let it sit for about 5-10 minutes, or until it becomes frothy.

2. Prepare the Dough:

   - In a large mixing bowl, combine the bread flour and salt. Make a well in the center and pour in the activated yeast mixture. Stir until a dough forms.

3. Knead the Dough:

   - Turn the dough out onto a floured surface. Knead for about 8-10 minutes, or until the dough becomes smooth and elastic.

4. First Rise:

   - Place the dough in a lightly oiled bowl, cover it with a clean kitchen towel, and let it rise in a warm place for 1-2 hours, or until it has doubled in size.

5. Shape the Loaves:

- Turn the dough out onto a floured surface and divide it into two equal portions. Shape each portion into a long baguette shape.

6. Second Rise:

    - Place the shaped loaves on a parchment-lined or lightly greased baking sheet, dusted with cornmeal. Cover them with a clean kitchen towel and let them rise for another 30-45 minutes.

7. Preheat the Oven:

    - Preheat your oven to 450°F (230°C).

8. Score the Loaves:

    - Use a sharp knife or razor blade to make diagonal slashes on the tops of the loaves.

9. Bake:

    - Bake in the preheated oven for 20-25 minutes, or until the loaves are golden brown and have a hollow sound when tapped on the bottom.

10. Cool:

    - Allow the New Orleans-Style French Bread to cool on a wire rack before slicing.

11. Enjoy:

    - Enjoy the authentic taste of New Orleans-Style French Bread as a side to your favorite dishes or for making traditional po'boy sandwiches.

This recipe yields two loaves of New Orleans-style French bread with a crispy crust and soft, airy interior. The technique and ingredients capture the essence of the iconic French bread found in New Orleans, perfect for savoring the flavors of Creole and Cajun cuisine. Whether used for sandwiches or served alongside classic Louisiana dishes, this bread is a delicious addition to any meal.

Cajun Cornbread

Ingredients:

- 1 cup yellow cornmeal
- 1 cup all-purpose flour
- 1 tablespoon baking powder
- 1/2 teaspoon baking soda
- 1 teaspoon salt
- 1 cup buttermilk
- 2 large eggs
- 1/4 cup unsalted butter, melted
- 1 cup corn kernels (fresh, frozen, or canned)
- 1/2 cup diced jalapeños (adjust to taste)
- 1 cup shredded cheddar cheese
- 1/2 cup green onions, chopped
- 1/4 cup fresh parsley, chopped
- 1/2 teaspoon cayenne pepper (adjust to taste)

Instructions:

1. Preheat the Oven:

   - Preheat your oven to 425°F (220°C). Grease a cast-iron skillet or a baking dish.

2. Mix Dry Ingredients:

   - In a large bowl, whisk together the yellow cornmeal, all-purpose flour, baking powder, baking soda, and salt.

3. Combine Wet Ingredients:

   - In another bowl, whisk together the buttermilk, eggs, and melted butter.

4. Combine Wet and Dry Ingredients:

   - Pour the wet ingredients into the dry ingredients and stir until just combined. Do not overmix.

5. Add Corn and Flavorings:

- Gently fold in the corn kernels, diced jalapeños, shredded cheddar cheese, green onions, chopped parsley, and cayenne pepper.

6. Pour into Skillet or Baking Dish:

    - Pour the batter into the greased skillet or baking dish, spreading it evenly.

7. Bake:

    - Bake in the preheated oven for 20-25 minutes or until the top is golden brown and a toothpick inserted into the center comes out clean.

8. Cool:

    - Allow the Cajun Cornbread to cool in the skillet or baking dish for a few minutes before slicing.

9. Serve:

    - Slice and serve the Cajun Cornbread as a flavorful side to your favorite Cajun or Creole dishes.

10. Enjoy:

    - Enjoy this moist and flavorful Cajun Cornbread, perfect for adding a spicy kick to your meal.

Cajun Cornbread is a delicious twist on the classic Southern staple, adding a touch of spice and flavor to your meal. Packed with corn, jalapeños, cheese, and Cajun seasonings, this cornbread is moist on the inside with a crispy crust. Serve it alongside gumbo, jambalaya, or any other Cajun or Creole dish for an authentic taste of Louisiana cuisine.

Sweet Potato Biscuits

Ingredients:

- 1 cup cooked and mashed sweet potatoes
- 1/2 cup unsalted butter, chilled and cubed
- 2 1/2 cups all-purpose flour
- 2 tablespoons brown sugar
- 1 tablespoon baking powder
- 1 teaspoon salt
- 1/2 teaspoon cinnamon
- 1/4 teaspoon nutmeg
- 3/4 cup buttermilk
- 1 tablespoon honey (for brushing)

Instructions:

1. Preheat the Oven:

   - Preheat your oven to 425°F (220°C). Line a baking sheet with parchment paper.

2. Prepare Sweet Potatoes:

   - Cook sweet potatoes until tender. Mash them thoroughly and let them cool.

3. Cut in Butter:

   - In a large bowl, combine the flour, brown sugar, baking powder, salt, cinnamon, and nutmeg. Add the chilled and cubed butter. Use a pastry cutter or your fingers to cut the butter into the dry ingredients until the mixture resembles coarse crumbs.

4. Add Mashed Sweet Potatoes:

   - Add the mashed sweet potatoes to the dry ingredients and butter mixture. Mix until just combined.

5. Pour in Buttermilk:

- Pour in the buttermilk and stir until the dough comes together. Be careful not to overmix.

6. Roll and Cut:

- Turn the dough out onto a floured surface. Gently knead it a few times, then roll it to about 1-inch thickness. Use a biscuit cutter to cut out biscuits and place them on the prepared baking sheet.

7. Bake:

- Bake in the preheated oven for 12-15 minutes or until the biscuits are golden brown.

8. Honey Glaze:

- While the biscuits are baking, warm honey slightly. Brush the baked biscuits with honey for a sweet glaze.

9. Cool:

- Allow the Sweet Potato Biscuits to cool on a wire rack for a few minutes before serving.

10. Enjoy:

- Serve these warm and flaky Sweet Potato Biscuits with a drizzle of honey for a delightful addition to breakfast or as a side to your favorite meal.

These Sweet Potato Biscuits are a wonderful twist on the classic biscuit, adding the natural sweetness and vibrant color of sweet potatoes. The combination of sweet and savory flavors, along with the hint of spices, makes these biscuits a perfect accompaniment to a variety of dishes. Whether served at breakfast or as a side during dinner, these biscuits are sure to be a hit.

King Cake

Ingredients:

For the Dough:

- 1 cup warm milk (110°F/43°C)
- 2 1/2 teaspoons active dry yeast (1 packet)
- 1/2 cup granulated sugar
- 4 cups all-purpose flour
- 1 teaspoon salt
- 1/2 teaspoon ground nutmeg
- 1/2 cup unsalted butter, softened
- 3 large eggs

For the Filling:

- 1/2 cup unsalted butter, softened
- 1 cup brown sugar, packed
- 2 tablespoons ground cinnamon

For the Icing:

- 2 cups powdered sugar
- 2-3 tablespoons milk
- 1/2 teaspoon vanilla extract
- Purple, green, and gold colored sugars (for decoration)

Instructions:

1. Activate the Yeast:

- In a small bowl, combine warm milk and 1 tablespoon of sugar. Sprinkle the yeast over the milk and let it sit for about 5-10 minutes, or until it becomes frothy.

2. Prepare Dough:

- In a large mixing bowl, combine the activated yeast mixture, remaining sugar, flour, salt, nutmeg, softened butter, and eggs. Mix until a dough forms.

3. Knead the Dough:

- Turn the dough out onto a floured surface and knead for about 8-10 minutes, or until it becomes smooth and elastic.

4. First Rise:

- Place the dough in a greased bowl, cover it with a clean kitchen towel, and let it rise in a warm place for about 1-2 hours, or until it has doubled in size.

5. Prepare Filling:

- In a small bowl, mix together the softened butter, brown sugar, and ground cinnamon to create the filling.

6. Roll and Fill:

- On a floured surface, roll out the dough into a large rectangle. Spread the filling evenly over the dough.

7. Roll into a Log:

- Roll the dough from the long side into a log. Seal the seam.

8. Shape the Ring:

- Form the log into a ring on a parchment-lined baking sheet. Pinch the ends together to seal.

9. Second Rise:

- Cover the shaped King Cake with a clean kitchen towel and let it rise for an additional 30-45 minutes.

10. Bake:

    - Preheat your oven to 350°F (175°C). Bake the King Cake for 25-30 minutes, or until it is golden brown.

11. Cool:

    - Allow the King Cake to cool on a wire rack.

12. Prepare Icing:

    - In a bowl, whisk together powdered sugar, milk, and vanilla extract to create the icing.

13. Decorate:

    - Once the King Cake has cooled, drizzle the icing over the top. Immediately sprinkle colored sugars in alternating sections of purple, green, and gold.

14. Enjoy:

    - Slice and enjoy this festive and delicious King Cake, a traditional treat for Mardi Gras celebrations.

King Cake is a festive and symbolic dessert enjoyed during Mardi Gras season. This sweet, cinnamon-filled cake is shaped into a ring and decorated with the vibrant colors of Mardi Gras – purple, green, and gold. Served as a centerpiece during celebrations, the person who finds the hidden trinket or baby inside is traditionally responsible for hosting the next King Cake party. This recipe captures the essence of this beloved New Orleans tradition.

Sauces and Condiments:

Remoulade Sauce

Ingredients:

- 1 cup mayonnaise
- 2 tablespoons Dijon mustard
- 1 tablespoon whole grain mustard
- 2 tablespoons ketchup
- 1 tablespoon Worcestershire sauce
- 1 tablespoon hot sauce (adjust to taste)
- 2 cloves garlic, minced
- 1 tablespoon capers, drained and chopped
- 1 tablespoon fresh parsley, finely chopped
- 1 tablespoon green onions, finely chopped
- 1 tablespoon lemon juice
- 1 teaspoon paprika
- Salt and black pepper to taste

Instructions:

1. Combine Ingredients:

   - In a bowl, whisk together mayonnaise, Dijon mustard, whole grain mustard, ketchup, Worcestershire sauce, hot sauce, minced garlic, capers, fresh parsley, green onions, lemon juice, and paprika.

2. Season:

   - Season the Remoulade Sauce with salt and black pepper to taste. Adjust the hot sauce according to your preferred level of spiciness.

3. Chill:

   - Cover the bowl with plastic wrap and refrigerate the Remoulade Sauce for at least 30 minutes before serving. This allows the flavors to meld.

4. Serve:

- Once chilled, give the sauce a final stir and serve it alongside your favorite dishes.

5. Enjoy:

- Enjoy this versatile Remoulade Sauce with seafood, po'boys, crab cakes, or as a zesty dipping sauce. It adds a burst of flavor to a variety of dishes.

Remoulade Sauce is a classic condiment with roots in French and Creole cuisine. This tangy and flavorful sauce pairs wonderfully with seafood, making it a popular choice for dishes like shrimp po'boys and crab cakes. With a combination of mayonnaise, mustard, ketchup, and various seasonings, Remoulade Sauce adds a zesty kick to elevate the taste of your favorite meals. Adjust the spice level and seasoning to suit your preferences.

Cajun Spice Mix

Ingredients:

- 2 tablespoons paprika
- 1 tablespoon garlic powder
- 1 tablespoon onion powder
- 1 tablespoon dried thyme
- 1 tablespoon dried oregano
- 1 tablespoon cayenne pepper (adjust to taste)
- 1 tablespoon ground black pepper
- 1 tablespoon white pepper
- 1 teaspoon dried basil
- 1 teaspoon dried parsley
- 1 teaspoon smoked paprika
- 1 teaspoon salt (adjust to taste)

Instructions:

1. Combine Ingredients:

- In a bowl, combine paprika, garlic powder, onion powder, dried thyme, dried oregano, cayenne pepper, ground black pepper, white pepper, dried basil, dried parsley, smoked paprika, and salt.

2. Mix Thoroughly:

- Mix the ingredients thoroughly to ensure an even distribution of flavors.

3. Store:

- Transfer the Cajun Spice Mix to an airtight container or a small jar with a tight-fitting lid.

4. Use:

- Use the Cajun Spice Mix as a seasoning for a variety of dishes, including Cajun and Creole recipes, grilled meats, seafood, vegetables, and more.

5. Adjust to Taste:

- Feel free to adjust the quantities of individual spices to suit your taste preferences. If you prefer more heat, you can increase the amount of cayenne pepper.

6. Enjoy:

- Sprinkle or rub the Cajun Spice Mix onto your favorite foods to add a burst of authentic Cajun flavor.

Cajun Spice Mix is a versatile blend that brings the bold and savory flavors of Cajun cuisine to your dishes. This homemade spice mix combines a variety of herbs and spices to create a well-balanced and aromatic seasoning. Use it to add depth and a touch of heat to your favorite recipes, whether you're grilling, sautéing, or seasoning a gumbo or jambalaya. Adjust the spice levels according to your taste preferences and enjoy the vibrant flavors of Cajun cooking.

Creole Mustard Sauce

Ingredients:

- 1/2 cup Creole mustard (or whole grain mustard)
- 2 tablespoons Dijon mustard
- 2 tablespoons mayonnaise
- 2 tablespoons white wine vinegar
- 1 clove garlic, minced
- 1 tablespoon honey
- 1 teaspoon Worcestershire sauce
- 1/2 teaspoon hot sauce (adjust to taste)
- Salt and black pepper to taste

Instructions:

1. Combine Mustards:

   - In a bowl, combine Creole mustard (or whole grain mustard) and Dijon mustard.

2. Add Remaining Ingredients:

   - Add mayonnaise, white wine vinegar, minced garlic, honey, Worcestershire sauce, and hot sauce to the mustards.

3. Mix Thoroughly:

   - Mix the ingredients thoroughly to ensure a smooth and well-blended sauce.

4. Season:

   - Season the Creole Mustard Sauce with salt and black pepper to taste. Adjust the hot sauce according to your preferred level of spiciness.

5. Refrigerate:

   - Cover the bowl with plastic wrap and refrigerate the Creole Mustard Sauce for at least 30 minutes before serving. This allows the flavors to meld.

6. Serve:

- Once chilled, give the sauce a final stir and serve it as a zesty condiment with a variety of dishes.

7. Enjoy:

- Enjoy this flavorful Creole Mustard Sauce as a dipping sauce, sandwich spread, or accompaniment to grilled meats and seafood.

Creole Mustard Sauce adds a tangy and zesty kick to your dishes, perfect for complementing the flavors of Cajun and Creole cuisine. Whether used as a dipping sauce, sandwich spread, or a flavorful addition to grilled meats and seafood, this sauce brings a burst of authentic Louisiana taste to your table. Adjust the spice level and seasoning to suit your preferences and enjoy the vibrant flavors of Creole cooking.

Hot Pepper Jelly

Ingredients:

- 1 cup finely diced bell peppers (red and green for color)
- 1/2 cup finely diced jalapeños (seeds and membranes removed for milder jelly)
- 1 1/2 cups apple cider vinegar
- 6 cups granulated sugar
- 1 packet liquid pectin
- 1/2 teaspoon butter (optional, to reduce foaming)
- Red food coloring (optional, for a more vibrant color)

Instructions:

1. Prepare Jars:

   - Sterilize your canning jars and lids by placing them in boiling water for 10 minutes. Keep them warm until ready to use.

2. Prepare Peppers:

   - Finely dice bell peppers and jalapeños. Use gloves when handling jalapeños to avoid irritation.

3. Combine Ingredients:

   - In a large pot, combine diced peppers, apple cider vinegar, and sugar. Stir well.

4. Bring to Boil:

   - Over medium-high heat, bring the mixture to a boil. Stir continuously to dissolve the sugar.

5. Add Pectin:

- Once boiling, add the liquid pectin and continue stirring. Add butter (optional) to reduce foaming.

6. Boil and Skim:

- Allow the mixture to boil for 1-2 minutes. Skim off any foam that rises to the surface.

7. Test for Gel:

- Perform a gel test by placing a small amount of the jelly on a cold plate. If it wrinkles when touched, it has reached the desired consistency.

8. Add Food Coloring:

- If desired, add a few drops of red food coloring to enhance the color of the jelly.

9. Fill Jars:

- Pour the hot pepper jelly into the prepared, warm jars, leaving about 1/4-inch headspace.

10. Seal Jars:

- Wipe the jar rims with a clean, damp cloth. Place sterilized lids on the jars and screw on the metal bands until fingertip-tight.

11. Process Jars:

- Process the jars in a boiling water bath for 5-10 minutes to ensure proper sealing.

12. Cool and Store:

- Allow the jars to cool completely. Check for proper seals by pressing down on the center of each lid. If it doesn't pop back, it's sealed. Store sealed jars in a cool, dark place.

13. Enjoy:

- Once cooled and sealed, you can enjoy your homemade Hot Pepper Jelly. It pairs well with crackers, cheese, or as a glaze for meats.

Hot Pepper Jelly adds a sweet and spicy kick to your dishes and makes for a delightful condiment or glaze. Whether served with cheese and crackers or used to enhance the flavor of meats, this homemade jelly brings a burst of flavor to your table. Adjust the heat level by modifying the amount of jalapeños, and feel free to experiment with different types of peppers for a unique twist on this classic jelly.

Blackened Seasoning

Ingredients:

- 2 tablespoons paprika
- 1 tablespoon dried thyme
- 1 tablespoon dried oregano
- 1 tablespoon onion powder
- 1 tablespoon garlic powder
- 1 tablespoon cayenne pepper
- 1 tablespoon ground black pepper
- 1 tablespoon white pepper
- 1 tablespoon smoked paprika
- 1 tablespoon salt

Instructions:

1. Combine Ingredients:

    - In a bowl, thoroughly combine paprika, dried thyme, dried oregano, onion powder, garlic powder, cayenne pepper, ground black pepper, white pepper, smoked paprika, and salt.

2. Mix Thoroughly:

    - Mix the ingredients well to ensure an even distribution of flavors.

3. Store:

    - Transfer the Blackened Seasoning to an airtight container or a spice jar with a tight-fitting lid.

4. Use:

    - Sprinkle or rub the Blackened Seasoning onto your favorite proteins, such as fish, chicken, or steak, before cooking.

5. Cooking Tips:

- When using Blackened Seasoning, heat a cast-iron skillet until very hot. Coat the protein with a small amount of oil, then generously rub the seasoning onto all sides. Cook the protein in the hot skillet until blackened, creating a flavorful crust.

6. Enjoy:

- Enjoy the bold and spicy flavors of Blackened Seasoning in your favorite dishes.

Blackened Seasoning is a robust and flavorful spice blend that adds depth and heat to a variety of dishes. It's particularly popular in Cajun and Creole cuisine, known for its bold and spicy flavors. Use this homemade Blackened Seasoning to create a blackened crust on proteins like fish, chicken, or steak, delivering a burst of authentic Louisiana taste to your meals. Adjust the heat level by modifying the amount of cayenne pepper to suit your preferences.

Desserts:

Bananas Foster

Ingredients:

- 4 ripe bananas, peeled and sliced diagonally
- 1/2 cup unsalted butter
- 1 cup brown sugar, packed
- 1/2 teaspoon ground cinnamon
- 1/4 cup banana liqueur
- 1/2 cup dark rum
- Vanilla ice cream (for serving)

Instructions:

1. Prepare Bananas:

- Peel the bananas and slice them diagonally into 1/2-inch thick pieces.

2. Melt Butter:

- In a large skillet or flambe pan, melt the butter over medium heat.

3. Add Brown Sugar and Cinnamon:

- Stir in the brown sugar and ground cinnamon, allowing the sugar to dissolve and the mixture to become smooth.

4. Cook Bananas:

- Add the sliced bananas to the skillet, gently stirring to coat them with the caramel sauce. Cook for 2-3 minutes until the bananas are slightly softened but not mushy.

5. Add Banana Liqueur:

- Carefully add the banana liqueur to the pan. Be cautious, as it may ignite. Allow the flame to subside.

6. Add Dark Rum:

- Pour in the dark rum and again, be cautious of any potential flames. Let it heat for a moment in the pan.

7. Flambe:

- Carefully ignite the alcohol by tilting the pan slightly. Allow the flames to subside naturally. If you're uncomfortable with the flambe, you can skip this step and simply let the alcohol cook off.

8. Serve:

- Spoon the bananas and sauce over vanilla ice cream in serving dishes.

9. Enjoy:

- Serve immediately and enjoy this classic New Orleans dessert!

Bananas Foster is a decadent and delicious dessert with a rich history rooted in New Orleans cuisine. The combination of caramelized bananas, brown sugar, and a touch of rum creates a flavorful and indulgent treat. Serve the warm banana mixture over a scoop of vanilla ice cream for a delightful contrast of temperatures and textures. The optional flambe step adds a dramatic touch to the preparation but can be skipped if desired. Whether you're celebrating a special occasion or just craving a sweet treat, Bananas Foster is sure to impress.

Beignets

Ingredients:

- 1 1/2 cups warm water (110°F/43°C)
- 1/2 cup granulated sugar
- 1 envelope (2 1/4 teaspoons) active dry yeast
- 4 cups all-purpose flour
- 1 cup evaporated milk
- 1/4 cup unsalted butter, melted
- 1 teaspoon vanilla extract
- 1/2 teaspoon salt
- Vegetable oil (for frying)
- Powdered sugar (for dusting)

Instructions:

1. Activate Yeast:

- In a bowl, combine warm water, sugar, and active dry yeast. Let it sit for 5-10 minutes until frothy.

2. Prepare Dough:

- In a large mixing bowl, combine the activated yeast mixture with flour, evaporated milk, melted butter, vanilla extract, and salt. Mix until a sticky dough forms.

3. Knead:

- Turn the dough out onto a floured surface and knead until smooth, adding more flour if needed. Place the dough in a greased bowl, cover with a damp cloth, and let it rise in a warm place for 2 hours or until doubled in size.

4. Roll and Cut:

- Roll the dough out to about 1/4-inch thickness on a floured surface. Cut into 2-inch squares.

5. Heat Oil:

- In a deep fryer or large, deep skillet, heat vegetable oil to 370°F (188°C).

6. Fry Beignets:

    - Fry the beignets in batches, flipping them until golden brown on both sides. This usually takes about 2-3 minutes per side.

7. Drain:

    - Remove the beignets from the oil using a slotted spoon and place them on paper towels to drain excess oil.

8. Dust with Powdered Sugar:

    - While still warm, generously dust the beignets with powdered sugar.

9. Serve:

    - Serve the beignets warm and enjoy this classic New Orleans treat!

Beignets are a beloved New Orleans delicacy, deep-fried dough squares that are crispy on the outside and soft on the inside, generously dusted with powdered sugar. These delightful treats are often enjoyed with a cup of coffee. Making beignets at home allows you to experience the joy of this iconic French Quarter treat anytime. Whether you're planning a Mardi Gras celebration or simply craving a sweet indulgence, beignets are sure to bring a taste of New Orleans to your kitchen.

Bread Pudding with Whiskey Sauce

Ingredients:

For the Bread Pudding:

- 6 cups stale French bread, torn into small pieces
- 2 cups whole milk
- 1 cup heavy cream
- 3/4 cup granulated sugar
- 4 large eggs, beaten
- 1/4 cup unsalted butter, melted
- 1 tablespoon vanilla extract
- 1/2 teaspoon ground cinnamon
- 1/4 teaspoon ground nutmeg
- 1/2 cup raisins (optional)

For the Whiskey Sauce:

- 1/2 cup unsalted butter
- 1/2 cup granulated sugar
- 1/2 cup brown sugar, packed
- 1/2 cup heavy cream
- 2 tablespoons whiskey (bourbon or your choice)

Instructions:

1. Preheat Oven:

- Preheat your oven to 350°F (175°C). Grease a 9x13-inch baking dish.

2. Prepare Bread Pudding:

- In a large bowl, combine torn French bread with milk and heavy cream. Let it soak for about 10 minutes.

3. Add Remaining Ingredients:

- To the soaked bread, add sugar, beaten eggs, melted butter, vanilla extract, ground cinnamon, ground nutmeg, and raisins (if using). Mix until well combined.

4. Bake:

- Pour the bread pudding mixture into the prepared baking dish. Bake in the preheated oven for 45-50 minutes or until the top is golden and the center is set.

5. Prepare Whiskey Sauce:

- While the bread pudding is baking, prepare the whiskey sauce. In a saucepan over medium heat, melt butter. Stir in granulated sugar, brown sugar, and heavy cream. Bring to a simmer and cook for 5 minutes, stirring frequently.

6. Add Whiskey:

- Remove the saucepan from heat and stir in the whiskey.

7. Serve:

- Once the bread pudding is baked, let it cool slightly before serving. Drizzle the warm whiskey sauce over individual servings.

8. Enjoy:

- Serve warm and enjoy the rich and comforting flavors of Bread Pudding with Whiskey Sauce.

Bread Pudding with Whiskey Sauce is a classic Southern dessert that combines the comforting warmth of bread pudding with the rich flavors of a decadent whiskey-infused sauce. This dessert is perfect for special occasions, holidays, or whenever you want to treat yourself to a delightful sweet indulgence. The combination of creamy bread pudding and the sweet and slightly boozy sauce creates a dessert that's both comforting and sophisticated.

Pralines

Ingredients:

- 1 cup granulated sugar
- 1 cup packed light brown sugar
- 1/2 cup unsalted butter
- 1/2 cup heavy cream
- 2 cups pecan halves
- 1 teaspoon vanilla extract

Instructions:

1. Prepare Baking Sheets:

- Line two baking sheets with parchment paper or silicone baking mats. Set aside.

2. Cook Sugar and Butter:

- In a heavy-bottomed saucepan over medium heat, combine granulated sugar, brown sugar, butter, and heavy cream. Stir until the butter is melted and the sugars are dissolved.

3. Bring to a Boil:

- Increase the heat to medium-high and bring the mixture to a boil, stirring constantly.

4. Cook to Soft-Ball Stage:

- Continue boiling and stirring until the mixture reaches the soft-ball stage (235°F to 240°F or 113°C to 116°C on a candy thermometer). This usually takes about 5-7 minutes.

5. Add Pecans:

- Remove the saucepan from heat and immediately stir in the pecan halves and vanilla extract.

6. Drop Pralines:

- Quickly drop spoonfuls of the praline mixture onto the prepared baking sheets. Work efficiently, as the mixture will start to set.

7. Let Cool:

- Allow the pralines to cool and harden at room temperature. This typically takes about 30 minutes.

8. Enjoy:

- Once the pralines are completely cooled and set, peel them off the parchment paper and enjoy these sweet, nutty treats.

Pralines are a classic Southern confection known for their sweet, creamy texture and rich pecan flavor. This homemade praline recipe allows you to recreate the delightful taste of this Southern treat in your own kitchen. With a perfect balance of sugar, butter, and pecans, these pralines make for a deliciously indulgent dessert or a thoughtful gift. Adjust the size of the pralines based on your preference, and savor the sweet, nutty goodness of this Southern delicacy.

Pecan Pie with Bourbon

Ingredients:

For the Pie Crust:

- 1 1/4 cups all-purpose flour
- 1/2 cup unsalted butter, chilled and cubed
- 1/4 cup granulated sugar
- 1/4 teaspoon salt
- 2-3 tablespoons ice water

For the Pecan Filling:

- 1 1/2 cups pecan halves
- 3 large eggs
- 1 cup light corn syrup
- 1/2 cup packed light brown sugar
- 1/4 cup unsalted butter, melted
- 2 tablespoons bourbon
- 1 teaspoon vanilla extract
- 1/4 teaspoon salt

Instructions:

1. Prepare Pie Crust:

- In a food processor, combine flour, chilled butter, sugar, and salt. Pulse until the mixture resembles coarse crumbs. Add ice water, one tablespoon at a time, and pulse until the dough comes together. Form the dough into a disc, wrap in plastic wrap, and refrigerate for at least 30 minutes.

2. Roll Out Crust:

- Preheat the oven to 375°F (190°C). Roll out the chilled pie crust on a floured surface and fit it into a 9-inch pie dish. Trim and crimp the edges.

3. Toast Pecans:

   - Toast the pecan halves in a dry skillet over medium heat for 3-5 minutes, stirring frequently. Remove from heat and set aside.

4. Prepare Pecan Filling:

   - In a bowl, whisk together eggs, corn syrup, brown sugar, melted butter, bourbon, vanilla extract, and salt until well combined.

5. Arrange Pecans:

   - Arrange the toasted pecan halves evenly over the pie crust.

6. Pour Filling:

   - Pour the pecan filling over the arranged pecans.

7. Bake:

   - Bake in the preheated oven for 40-45 minutes or until the filling is set. If the crust edges start to brown too quickly, cover them with aluminum foil.

8. Cool:

   - Allow the pecan pie to cool completely before slicing.

9. Serve:

   - Serve slices of pecan pie at room temperature and enjoy the rich, bourbon-infused flavors.

10. Optional:

- Optionally, serve with a dollop of whipped cream or a scoop of vanilla ice cream for an extra treat.

Pecan Pie with Bourbon adds a delightful twist to the classic pecan pie, infusing it with the rich and warm flavors of bourbon. The combination of toasty pecans, a gooey filling, and a buttery crust makes this dessert a perfect addition to holiday tables or any special occasion. Whether enjoyed on its own or with a dollop of whipped cream, this pecan pie is sure to be a crowd-pleaser.

King Cake Cheesecake

Ingredients:

For the Crust:

- 1 1/2 cups graham cracker crumbs
- 1/4 cup melted unsalted butter
- 1/4 cup granulated sugar

For the Cheesecake Filling:

- 4 (8-ounce) packages cream cheese, softened
- 1 1/4 cups granulated sugar
- 1/2 cup sour cream
- 1/4 cup all-purpose flour
- 4 large eggs
- 1 teaspoon vanilla extract
- 1/2 teaspoon almond extract

For the Cinnamon Sugar Swirl:

- 1/4 cup granulated sugar
- 1 tablespoon ground cinnamon

For the Icing:

- 2 cups powdered sugar
- 2-3 tablespoons milk
- 1/2 teaspoon vanilla extract
- Purple, green, and gold colored sugars (for decoration)

Instructions:

1. Preheat Oven:

    - Preheat your oven to 325°F (163°C). Grease a 9-inch springform pan.

2. Make the Crust:

- In a bowl, combine graham cracker crumbs, melted butter, and granulated sugar. Press the mixture into the bottom of the prepared springform pan to form the crust.

3. Prepare Cheesecake Filling:

    - In a large mixing bowl, beat cream cheese until smooth. Add granulated sugar, sour cream, flour, eggs, vanilla extract, and almond extract. Mix until well combined and smooth.

4. Create Cinnamon Sugar Swirl:

    - In a small bowl, mix together granulated sugar and ground cinnamon to create the cinnamon sugar swirl.

5. Assemble Cheesecake:

    - Pour half of the cheesecake batter over the crust. Sprinkle half of the cinnamon sugar swirl over the batter. Repeat with the remaining batter and swirl mixture.

6. Bake:

    - Bake in the preheated oven for 60-70 minutes or until the center is set. If the top starts to brown too quickly, cover it loosely with aluminum foil.

7. Cool:

    - Allow the cheesecake to cool in the pan for about 15 minutes, then run a knife around the edge to loosen it. Let it cool completely before refrigerating.

8. Make Icing:

    - In a bowl, whisk together powdered sugar, milk, and vanilla extract to create the icing. Adjust the consistency by adding more milk if needed.

9. Decorate:

    - Once the cheesecake is fully cooled, spread the icing over the top. Immediately sprinkle colored sugars in alternating sections of purple, green, and gold.

10. Chill:

- Refrigerate the cheesecake for at least 4 hours or overnight before serving.

11. Enjoy:

- Slice and enjoy this festive King Cake Cheesecake, a delightful twist on the traditional Mardi Gras treat.

King Cake Cheesecake combines the flavors of the iconic King Cake with the creamy richness of a classic cheesecake. With a graham cracker crust, a cinnamon sugar swirl, and vibrant colored sugar decorations, this dessert is a festive addition to Mardi Gras celebrations. The almond and vanilla extracts add a depth of flavor reminiscent of the traditional King Cake. Serve this cheesecake to family and friends to bring a taste of New Orleans to your Mardi Gras festivities.

Creole Cream Cheese Ice Cream

Ingredients:

- 2 cups Creole cream cheese
- 1 cup whole milk
- 1 cup heavy cream
- 3/4 cup granulated sugar
- 1 teaspoon vanilla extract
- Pinch of salt

Instructions:

1. Prepare Creole Cream Cheese:

    - If you can't find Creole cream cheese at your local store, you can make your own by combining 2 cups of whole milk with 2 tablespoons of buttermilk. Let it sit at room temperature for 12-24 hours until it thickens and develops a tangy flavor.

2. Mix Ingredients:

    - In a bowl, whisk together Creole cream cheese, whole milk, heavy cream, granulated sugar, vanilla extract, and a pinch of salt until well combined.

3. Chill Mixture:

    - Cover the bowl and refrigerate the mixture for at least 4 hours or overnight to allow the flavors to meld and the mixture to chill thoroughly.

4. Churn Ice Cream:

    - Transfer the chilled mixture to an ice cream maker and churn according to the manufacturer's instructions until it reaches a soft-serve consistency.

5. Freeze:

    - Transfer the churned ice cream to a lidded container and freeze for an additional 4 hours or until firm.

6. Serve:

- Scoop the Creole Cream Cheese Ice Cream into bowls or cones and serve.

7. Enjoy:

- Enjoy the unique and delicious flavors of Creole cream cheese in this homemade ice cream. Garnish with fresh berries or a drizzle of honey for an extra treat.

Creole Cream Cheese Ice Cream celebrates the distinct and tangy flavor of Creole cream cheese, a traditional ingredient in Louisiana cuisine. This homemade ice cream is rich, creamy, and showcases the unique characteristics of Creole cream cheese. Enjoy it on its own or as a delightful accompaniment to your favorite desserts. Whether you're a fan of the Creole cream cheese tradition or just looking to try something new, this ice cream is a delicious and refreshing treat.

Sweet Potato Pie

Ingredients:

For the Pie Crust:

- 1 1/4 cups all-purpose flour
- 1/2 cup unsalted butter, chilled and cubed
- 1/4 cup granulated sugar
- 1/4 teaspoon salt
- 3-4 tablespoons ice water

For the Sweet Potato Filling:

- 2 cups mashed sweet potatoes (about 3 medium sweet potatoes)
- 3/4 cup granulated sugar
- 1/2 cup packed light brown sugar
- 1/2 cup unsalted butter, melted
- 1/2 cup evaporated milk
- 3 large eggs
- 1 teaspoon vanilla extract
- 1/2 teaspoon ground cinnamon
- 1/4 teaspoon ground nutmeg
- 1/4 teaspoon salt

Instructions:

1. Preheat Oven:

- Preheat your oven to 375°F (190°C).

2. Make Pie Crust:

- In a food processor, combine flour, chilled butter, sugar, and salt. Pulse until the mixture resembles coarse crumbs. Add ice water, one tablespoon at a time, and pulse until the dough comes together. Form the dough into a disc, wrap in plastic wrap, and refrigerate for at least 30 minutes.

3. Roll Out Crust:

- Roll out the chilled pie crust on a floured surface and fit it into a 9-inch pie dish. Trim and crimp the edges.

4. Prepare Sweet Potatoes:

- Peel, cube, and boil sweet potatoes until tender. Mash them and measure out 2 cups.

5. Make Filling:

- In a large bowl, combine mashed sweet potatoes, granulated sugar, brown sugar, melted butter, evaporated milk, eggs, vanilla extract, ground cinnamon, ground nutmeg, and salt. Mix until well combined.

6. Assemble Pie:

- Pour the sweet potato filling into the prepared pie crust.

7. Bake:

- Bake in the preheated oven for 45-50 minutes or until the center is set and a knife inserted into the center comes out clean.

8. Cool:

- Allow the sweet potato pie to cool completely on a wire rack.

9. Serve:

- Once cooled, slice and serve. Optionally, top with whipped cream for an extra treat.

10. Enjoy:

- Enjoy the comforting flavors of homemade Sweet Potato Pie, a classic dessert perfect for holidays and family gatherings.

Sweet Potato Pie is a Southern classic known for its rich and creamy filling with warm spices. This recipe combines a buttery pie crust with a luscious sweet potato filling, creating a delightful dessert that's perfect for any occasion. Whether served at

Thanksgiving, Christmas, or a simple family dinner, this Sweet Potato Pie is sure to be a hit. Customize it with a dollop of whipped cream or a sprinkle of cinnamon for an extra touch of sweetness.

Cajun Apple Dumplings

Ingredients:

For the Dumplings:

- 2 large Granny Smith apples, peeled, cored, and cut into quarters
- 1 can (8 ounces) crescent roll dough
- 1/2 cup unsalted butter, melted
- 1/2 cup granulated sugar
- 1 teaspoon ground cinnamon

For the Sauce:

- 1 cup granulated sugar
- 1 cup water
- 1/2 cup unsalted butter
- 1/2 teaspoon ground cinnamon
- 1/4 teaspoon ground nutmeg

Instructions:

1. Preheat Oven:

- Preheat your oven to 350°F (175°C).

2. Prepare Dumplings:

- Roll each apple quarter in a crescent roll triangle, starting from the wider end. Place the wrapped apples in a greased baking dish.

3. Make Cinnamon Sugar Coating:

- In a small bowl, combine melted butter, granulated sugar, and ground cinnamon.

4. Coat Dumplings:

- Brush the crescent-wrapped apples with the cinnamon sugar mixture, making sure to coat them evenly.

5. Bake:

- Bake in the preheated oven for 30-35 minutes or until the dumplings are golden brown and cooked through.

6. Prepare Sauce:

- While the dumplings are baking, prepare the sauce. In a saucepan, combine granulated sugar, water, butter, ground cinnamon, and ground nutmeg. Bring the mixture to a boil, stirring until the sugar is dissolved.

7. Pour Sauce Over Dumplings:

- Once the dumplings are out of the oven, pour the hot sauce over them, ensuring each dumpling is coated.

8. Serve:

- Allow the Cajun Apple Dumplings to cool for a few minutes before serving.

9. Enjoy:

- Serve warm, either on their own or with a scoop of vanilla ice cream for an extra treat.

Cajun Apple Dumplings offer a unique twist on the classic dessert by incorporating warm spices and a rich sauce. This recipe combines the sweetness of baked apples with the flakiness of crescent roll dough, creating a comforting and flavorful treat. The Cajun-inspired sauce adds a delightful touch of spice to complement the sweetness of the dumplings. Whether served as a dessert for a special occasion or a cozy family dinner, these Cajun Apple Dumplings are sure to be a hit with your taste buds.

Bourbon Street Chocolate Pecan Pie

Ingredients:

For the Pie Crust:

- 1 1/4 cups all-purpose flour
- 1/2 cup unsalted butter, chilled and cubed
- 1/4 cup granulated sugar
- 1/4 teaspoon salt
- 3-4 tablespoons ice water

For the Chocolate Pecan Filling:

- 1 cup semisweet chocolate chips
- 1 1/2 cups pecan halves
- 3 large eggs
- 1 cup light corn syrup
- 1/2 cup packed light brown sugar
- 1/4 cup unsalted butter, melted
- 2 tablespoons bourbon
- 1 teaspoon vanilla extract
- 1/4 teaspoon salt

Instructions:

1. Preheat Oven:

- Preheat your oven to 350°F (175°C).

2. Make Pie Crust:

- In a food processor, combine flour, chilled butter, sugar, and salt. Pulse until the mixture resembles coarse crumbs. Add ice water, one tablespoon at a time, and pulse until the dough comes together. Form the dough into a disc, wrap in plastic wrap, and refrigerate for at least 30 minutes.

3. Roll Out Crust:

- Roll out the chilled pie crust on a floured surface and fit it into a 9-inch pie dish. Trim and crimp the edges.

4. Prepare Chocolate Pecan Filling:

- Sprinkle the chocolate chips evenly over the bottom of the pie crust. In a bowl, combine pecan halves, eggs, corn syrup, brown sugar, melted butter, bourbon, vanilla extract, and salt. Mix until well combined.

5. Assemble Pie:

- Pour the pecan mixture over the chocolate chips in the pie crust.

6. Bake:

- Bake in the preheated oven for 50-60 minutes or until the center is set and a knife inserted into the center comes out clean. If the crust edges start to brown too quickly, cover them with aluminum foil.

7. Cool:

- Allow the Bourbon Street Chocolate Pecan Pie to cool completely on a wire rack.

8. Serve:

- Once cooled, slice and serve. Optionally, top with whipped cream or a scoop of vanilla ice cream for an extra treat.

9. Enjoy:

- Enjoy the rich and indulgent flavors of Bourbon Street Chocolate Pecan Pie, a delightful dessert perfect for special occasions or a decadent treat.

Bourbon Street Chocolate Pecan Pie combines the classic pecan pie with the rich and decadent addition of chocolate and a hint of bourbon. This dessert is perfect for those who enjoy a delightful fusion of flavors in their pie. The buttery and flaky crust, the gooey pecan filling, and the luscious layer of chocolate make this pie a showstopper on any dessert table. Serve it during the holidays or as a special treat for chocolate and pecan pie enthusiasts.

www.ingramcontent.com/pod-product-compliance
Lightning Source LLC
LaVergne TN
LVHW081551060526
838201LV00054B/1856